I'm OK!
I'm just not finished

A Handbook for Empowerment

2nd Edition

L. Cameron Mosher, Ph.D.

P.O. Box 331, Sandy, Utah 84091
801-243-7404
Empowerment Tools (dba of Cam Mosher and Associates, Inc.)

DEDICATION

To my father, Hugh Cameron Mosher,

who showed me the inner-directed life,

And to his mother, Cora Estelle Cameron,

who inspired me to a love of nature.

Table of Contents

Section One—
The Map

Introduction

The Map

The Principles

The Beginnings of My Journey

Introduction—

One of the most powerful book titles I know is "Everything I Need to Know I Learned in Kindergarten" by Robert Fulghum. The title tells it like it is. Life is not complicated. The principles on which a satisfying, empowered life experience is based are very simple. In my quarter century of experience as a facilitator for personal and team development, I have come to believe that most people haven't a clue how simple the principles are nor how to build a satisfying life upon them. They get caught up in the details of living, focused on the circumstances of their lives, and conclude that they have limited power to change their experience of life. They live as victims, their experience determined by things outside of them: their spouse, their boss, their children, their physical conditions, or their circumstances.

There are a lot of "positive mental attitude" approaches to personal empowerment. This is not one of them. Empowerment is not about hyping yourself up. It is about choosing to base your life on a few simple but profound principles, to live in the present moment, and to shift your perceptions of the world out of the past and into the present. It is about letting yourself grow up (not living in the past) and putting the magnificent adult that you are in charge of your life. From this new perspective, you will experience control over your life, direction and purpose, confidence and self-esteem, satisfaction in your relationships, and a sense of inner peace. This comes with the territory of Empowerment!

Let's define **Empowerment** as it applies to living a satisfying life. *Empowerment is a Realization and a Decision.*

Empowerment is the <u>realization</u> that I control my own life experience and that I choose how I live and how I respond to everything. I choose how I deal with every circumstance in my life, including every unpleasant or unfortunate circumstance.

Empowerment is the <u>decision</u> that I have the resources to deal with every challenge. I am the captain of my life and I find positive value in everything I encounter. I am bigger than any circumstance!

Does that sound like a tall order? To most people, who may see themselves as victims in life, it is beyond comprehension. But you have a choice, a decision to make. You either choose to incorporate empowerment into your life, or you choose to allow circumstances and other people to control your feelings and choices like a puppet on a string. Victimhood is the default choice. That's it! *You* can decide today. One or the other. Empowerment or victimhood. In fact, you make that choice every day, and in every circumstance whether you show up Empowered or as a victim. Until you choose to be Empowered, you get the default choice that you are a victim of things that you believe are out of your control. It's truly that simple. You make a conscious choice for Empowerment or an unconscious agreement for victimhood. You cannot be both. Which choice will give you the results that serve your highest good and purposes? Are you getting the results you want thus far in life? Why not commit to Empowerment today? It's your life and your decision.

Now let's define **Satisfaction, which goes hand in hand with Empowerment, and is simply a result of your Empowerment realization,** *and a second decision.*

Satisfaction is not necessarily "happiness" or "comfort". One may be in pain or stress or struggle and yet experience satisfaction. Satisfaction results from the empowering <u>realization</u> that you <u>are</u> in charge of your life **AND** *from the decision that you <u>stand for something</u>: that you are true to your values and principles, that you do not "sell out" to lesser things that are not your higher truth, and that life is good and you are good.* This is congruent living.

Note that second part! An Empowered Life results in Satisfaction, as a natural outcome of that second decision, that you stand for something, which increases self-esteem.

Those of us who are determined to take charge of our lives by living in congruence, live simple but profoundly meaningful principles that bring empowerment and satisfaction. These principles find universal expression in different philosophies and diverse languages. I am drawn to Native American philosophies and ceremonies, because I recognize these simple Principles of Growth and Empowerment within the symbols and metaphors of Native American Medicine. The

Medicine Wheel—The Circle of Four Directions—is a sacred tradition or mechanism for illustrating the principles and the processes of healing and transforming life. Such traditions become maps for guiding us to and through the Journey to an Empowered Life.

I follow the Red Path spiritually, despite the fact that I am not of indigenous Native American ancestry (I am of Celt descent). The language of the Red Path, particularly the Medicine Circle, resonates within me. What follows are my interpretations of the Sacred Circle for the purposes of this book. They are not intended to represent any particular tribe or Native culture.

In the Medicine Wheel, the Four Directions form the basic framework for much of Native American spiritual thought and ritual. The directions and their related symbols, creatures, and colors have been useful to me in my personal understanding of the process of healing, transformation, and Empowerment in life. Accordingly, I begin this book with an illustration of the Sacred Medicine Circle, as I appreciate and comprehend it. I present my understanding as a *map* of the process of healing and empowerment, and invite you to return to this presentation of the Sacred Circle frequently as you read this book. By returning to this section, you will be supported in further developing your own metaphorical and symbolic map of life, as well as in more fully examining your own personal beliefs and life patterns, and how those patterns may or may not support your journey to true enlightenment in all areas of your life. Are you getting the results you want? Is your life journey joyful? Are you standing in your personal power? How much happiness can you stand?

The Map—

The Medicine Circle as a Map of the Journey of Transformation

Smoke from the small fire spiraled up toward the hole at the top of the tipi, driven by fresh air coming in through the open door. The first shafts of the rising sun shone through the door of the lodge and fell on the face of the Elder who sat quietly, filling the bowl of his pipe with sacred tobacco. The early light illuminated the circle of young men who waited for the Storyteller to begin.

Taking a glowing stick from the fire, he lit the pipe. As the sacred smoke rose from his pipe, he took an eagle feather and wafted it around the circle toward the faces of the boys as a cleansing smudge. Looking slowly at each face around the circle, he began to speak, his words and actions carrying the ancient tradition passed to him by generations of Storytellers before him. His duty and responsibility was to teach the youth of his tribe the Map of the Journey of Transformation and Healing in Life as contained in the ancient symbol of the Medicine Circle, the Circle of Four Directions. This was a moment of great importance for the young men before him as they committed to memory this simple, yet profound guide to living an empowered life.

The East

"Look out at the sun," he began. "It rises in the East, the place of beginnings. It comes up over the mountain and illuminates the dark places here in the valley. Even now, it shines through the door of our lodge, the door where you entered today, and illuminates the opportunity each of us has to examine life and its opportunities to learn and grow. Learn from this that the challenges of life are our greatest illuminators. They show us our issues and what we must address to transform and heal as we move upward in life."

He paused, picked up the eagle feather again, and continued, "Our brother the Eagle is a creature of the East. As the sun rises in the East, eagle rises with it, a creature of the day. Eagle soars on the rising currents of air heated by the sun. Eagle Medicine is the medicine of Spirit. Eagle comes as a Messenger of Spirit, to fly with us throughout the journey around the Circle, to keep reminding us that the Healing Journey is a Spiritual Journey. Eagle also rises in the East to give us Courage, the courage to face the issues of our lives and not shrink back. Eagle cries out that we must not avoid or quit, but confront, and find the courage to walk the entire Circle." The old man took from his bundle a massive Eagle Talon with its sharp claws, and holding it up, the Elder looked around the circle. Each young man knew what courage it takes to face that talon, the Eagle Talon that pierces flesh in the Sun Dance.

The old man went on, "Each direction has a color. Each color gives meaning and power to the circle. You must pay attention to all the colors, for together they bring special meaning to the whole."

"The color of the East is Red. It is the color of the clouds as they are painted by the sun in the morning, at the beginning of the day cycle. It is the color of many flowers as they come up in the springtime, the beginning of the year cycle. It is the color of blood, associated with birth at the beginning of the life cycle."

With that the Storyteller got up, carefully holding his pipe, cradling the precious stone bowl in the cup of his hand, resting the wooden stem on his forearm, and moved sunwise around the circle, past the east door, stopping in front of the boy seated in the south. Taking it deftly with his fingers from the leather pouch around his neck, he placed a juniper berry in the young man's mouth.

The South

"My son," he began, "the South is the place of youth. It is the place of knowledge. Even as you chew on the juniper berry and explore its flavors, so the South is the place where you explore and learn of the basic skills of life. A creature of the South is Wolf, the Teacher!"

Taking a piece of fur from his pouch, he rubbed it softly on the face of the boy. "This is Wolf. He will teach you of causes and effects. With Wolf, you will learn how you have drawn conclusions about yourself and about your life in your infancy and childhood. Wolf will show you how these infantile conclusions influence your perception of reality and direct your life through adulthood! Unless you follow this map and walk this circle, spiraling ever upward with each pass around its teachings and experiences, you are doomed to have your inner child run your life forever, even as an adult!"

Moving to the next boy in the south of the circle, the Storyteller continued, "Another creature of the South is Porcupine. Porcupine Medicine is the medicine of youth, of Trust and Innocence." He drew a small object from the back of his sleeve and poked the quill into the forehead of the startled boy. Leaving it imbedded there, he declared to all in the circle, "But porcupine has quills only on its back. It has no quills on its belly. The belly of the Porcupine is its vulnerable place. The predators of Porcupine attack it in its belly, in its place of vulnerability. In the Healing Circle, the South is the Place of Vulnerability!"

Looking down at the wide-eyed youth, he explained, "Each of us has erected a wall in our lives. It is called the Wall of Shame and Guilt. Behind that wall, we try to hide all the stuff that we believe condemns us. But Porcupine says, if you want to heal your guilt and shame, you must come out from behind that wall and be Vulnerable. You must reveal the hidden stuff! You see, Porcupine reminds us that we are all human. Porcupine invites you to rejoin the human race. You must accept and reveal your humanity to rejoin the human race!

Human Beings have both Strengths *AND* Weaknesses. Our weaknesses do not condemn us. They show us our opportunities to learn and grow. Porcupine teaches you to accept your humanity by being willing to consider it, own it, and reveal it!"

The Storyteller slowly turned around, looking each boy directly in the eye, and declared, "Your Creator does not look upon you with condemnation. It is only *you* who have decided in your arrogance that you are unworthy, that you must be superhuman and have no weaknesses! Decide again, right now, that it is okay to be you, with all your weaknesses, and accept yourself as Child of your Creator, a *magnificent* human being. Commit yourself to continue the journey of healing and growth around the circle, traveling on with Eagle, Wolf, and Porcupine, to seek the healing place in the North."

Looking down at the quill still embedded in the boy's forehead, the Storyteller took the quill in his fingers and yanked it out. The boy winced as the barbs gripped his flesh and then gave way under the old man's brisk pull. A tiny bead of blood appeared where the quill had been. Seeing the blood, the Storyteller went on, "Red is in the East and that comes first in the circle, but the circle advances to the South where the color is Yellow. It is the color of the sun at noontime in the day cycle. It is the color of the corn and squash ripening in the summer fields in the year cycle. It is the color of the radiance that beams from the face of the innocent child in the life cycle." He licked his thumb and gently wiped the drop of blood from the boy's forehead. With a gentle tousle of the boy's hair, he smiled at him with love and acceptance.

The West

Slowly turning all the way around, Storyteller looked again into each boy's eyes, then stepped back to where he had first been seated opposite the door. Remaining standing, he said, "This is the West, the place of Maturity. Here we see balance taught by the Circle. Each side of the Circle is balanced by a correspondence on the opposite side." Reaching inside his shirt, he draws out a forked pine bough. "A forked stick in the West represents male and female coming together to form family. Procreation takes place in the West. Birth takes place in the East. You must pay close attention to the balance of the Circle. It is important to find balance in your life. If you put too much emphasis on only some parts of your life and interests, you will get your life out of balance and roll down life's journey bumpy!"

Leaning forward, he lowered his voice, "Now listen carefully. A creature of the West is Bear. Bear hibernates half the year in the cave. When Bear wakes up, he calls to us from within the cave."

"WAKE UP!" he shouted, startling the boys. "It is like we have been hibernating half our lives. It is time in the West to wake up and go into the cave of our life and do the work of healing and growth!"

With squinting eyes, the old man peered down at his young charges. His voice thundered! "In the East, our issues are illuminated. In the South, we reveal them and talk about them. In the West, we go into the cave of our life and deal with them! Bear Medicine is the Medicine of Looks Within, the Medicine of Introspection. You have come to that time of your life, the time for you to go into the West cave and prepare for manhood!"

He paused silently for some time allowing his words to sink in, and then continued. Storyteller explained, "We go with Bear into the west cave and there we meet Crow. Crow is very important to you. His is the Medicine of Inner Law. Crow Medicine tells you what drives your choices. With Crow you see your motives. Crow shows you how, down inside, you set your whole life up. Your life is just as you created it."

Now the Storyteller's voice becomes very intense as he speaks of listening to the inner law. "Crow asks you some questions. You must learn to listen to your answers within! The first question is: What is the form of the inner law that drives your choices? How does it sound in your mind and heart as it exercises control over your choices? If it has the form '*SUPPOSED TO*,' then you know it comes from *outside you.* It is the law of others."

"Crow then asks, who told you that you were *Supposed To*? With Bear you introspect. You learn to look inside you, to recognize your inner voice and inspect it. Hah, you say, government, society, culture told me. Or religion told me. Or family told me. Finally you recognize that the original voice of *Supposed To* was your mother. She was the first human being with whom you had intimate contact. You were dependent on her for everything in the womb. Then you were mostly dependent on her for the first few years of your life. The basic foundation of your entire life perception was formed in that dependency. With your mother you learned to subconsciously subjugate yourself to authority. Wolf is even now showing you causes and effects!"

Crow then tells you of another form of your inner law, *Want To*. Want to comes from *inside you.* Crow then asks you what do *you* want? What desires come from within yourself? Can you recognize that form? Really? Or have you become so used to living the "supposed to" law that you only see what you believe you are supposed to want?

The boys were beginning to squirm. They had begun to feel pride in their approaching manhood. Now they realized the Elder considered them still pretty juvenile. They realized the kinds of desires that were raging in their pubescent minds and bodies. And they knew what their parents and others had told them they were supposed to do about them.

The Elder squinted his eyes and, looking around the circle, seemed to drill them into the eyes of each boy. "With Crow you must learn the critical Law of Respect. You see, Crow teaches Boundaries. Crow says that the empowered inner law is not driven by desires. One learns to love and respect self. In that spirit of self-respect, one says to self, 'Just because I want this, I see that it might be disrespectful to me, perhaps harmful to me, to partake of it. Therefore, out of respect for myself, I will turn aside from it. I must set boundaries for myself based on love and respect for myself!'"

The boys knew in their hearts what the Elder would say next. Storyteller continued, "That love and respect of self provides an inner framework, an inner guide, for your relations with others. Crow tells you that just because you may Desire To with respect to another person, because you have an inner framework of self-respect, you can also apply that to the other person, even if that person does not have such an inner framework for her or himself. Just because you Desire To, does not mean you must Choose To! Your own inner framework of love and respect guides you to love and respect the other equally. True Want To comes from an inner truth that may override Desire To. Honoring an inner Truth is the sign of True Manhood! Crow teaches you of True Character."

The Elder continued on. "The West cave is a pretty serious place. Deeper in the cave, deep where Bear and Crow lead you, you must face Owl!" He knelt down and opened a leather bundle at his feet and lifted up a magnificent pair of wings. Holding them spread wide in his hands, he declared, "These are the wings of Owl. They are raptor wings! But they are not designed to soar high on the air heated by the sun, as are the wings of Eagle." Moving slowly around the circle, he rubbed the cheek of each boy with the soft feathers of the wings. "Owl wings are soft. Owl flies silently. Owl hunts up close."

He bent down and took a small staff from the bundle. On its tip was mounted the head of a small Owl. Turning the staff in his hands he went on, "Owl eyes are as keen as Eagle's, though not to see from high in the sky. Owl is a creature of the night. Owl eyes are designed to see close up, in the dark." Bending down, he took another small object from his bundle. Holding the Owl talon in the light of the fire and speaking almost in a whisper, he said, "Owl comes into your life silently, into the dark places, talons extended. Owl comes in the pains and struggles of life, the challenges and adversities. But Owl does not come to destroy you. He comes to get your attention! You see, Owl medicine is the medicine of Deception."

Pausing to let that sink in, he continued, "Owl comes not to deceive you, but to get your attention to *how you deceive yourself!* And what is that great deception by which you deceive yourself? It is your Belief System, that set of conclusions and beliefs derived by you from your experiences since infancy and early childhood, and through which you define and perceive your reality. Owl challenges that set of conclusions and beliefs that filter what is real into your perception of it!" His voiced thundered as he spoke this great truth: "The greatest deception of all is that you actually believe *you are right in your perception!* Owl's talons will continue to visit you so long as you insist that your beliefs and perceptions are the only ones; so long as you stay stuck in the Arrogance of Being Right! Your journey with Owl will be a painful one, and your insistence on Being Right will only prolong the pain!"

The boys sat in silence, contemplating what the Elder had said. They well knew how they argued and fought with each other, and how they resisted their parents' counsel, to prove how right they were. To the boys, it seemed so important to Be Right! How would they have an identity if it could not be based on the Rightness of Ego?

The Elder reached down and picked up the forked stick again to emphasize a point. "In the West, we see balance taught in the circle. A forked stick in the West represents male and female coming together to form family. Procreation takes place in the West. Birth takes place in the East. Each side of the circle is balanced by corresponding things on the other side. Innocence in the East. Ego in the West. Are we bumping down the path of life out of balance?"

"Ah the color of the West!" declared the Elder. "How appropriate! It is Black. It is the color of the falling night. It is the color of the leaves as they fall from the trees in the Fall of the year and decay. It is the color of Death! But it is in the West, the prime of life. It is not the death of the body." He paused and said in a low, slow voice, *"It is the death of the Deception!"*

The boys shrank inward as they realized the powerful truth of the Elder's words, the wisdom that came with his age and experience. Each boy had a foreboding that he would discover through the pains of life's lessons that his deceived ego-man must struggle and die in order for him to discover and appreciate his true self. The pride of their young manhood would be painful, until Wisdom was forged by many encounters with Owl. Owl medicine would be their medicine of Ultimate Truth! Owl medicine would bring wisdom, and the price they would pay would show with the snowy hair of age and experience.

The North

The white haired old man looked around at his young charges. He remembered well how sure he had been of himself at that young age, how much he thought he knew about life. He remembered how he had scoffed at the counsel of his father and mother and the elders, confident in his adolescence that he had all the answers. Ah, how Owl had taught him of his arrogance!

Standing tall with his white hair glistening in the full sunlight streaming through the lodge door, he walked to the North side of the circle. "This is the North, the place of Wisdom," he declared. "Again balance is taught by the circle. The knowledge gained in the South of Life must pass through the encounters with Bear, Crow, and Owl in the West before it becomes Wisdom in the North!"

Each of the young men looked down, hiding their eyes from the piercing stare of the Elder as he continued. "You know how you have been taught by your grandfathers and grandmothers. Your parents have been out making the living that has sustained you. They have been out hunting, preparing your food and clothing, repairing your lodge, while the white haired ones, the grandparents who have gained wisdom through their experiences of life, taught you how to read the signs and learn the traditions and teachings of our ancestors."

He paused for a moment, thinking of his encounters with the white man's culture. "The white men have it all wrong," he said. "They send their elders away to nursing homes. Their children move away from the parents taking the grandchildren with them. They have separated the generations. Their teachers are not much older or experienced than those they teach. Their teachers focus on pure knowledge divorced from life experience! Their youth are disconnected from the wisdom of their elders, from the things they have learned as a culture that bring meaning and stability to life. Their young people float, trying to find their connections through drugs, alcohol, and sex. No wonder the white world, and many of the other so-called 'civilized' cultures, are falling apart! They have lost the anchors of true Wisdom, the Wisdom that only comes through cultural experience passed down from generation to generation by the elders!"

The young men knew why it was so important that this ritual always takes place at adolescence for each generation and why they were sitting at the feet of this wise old man. They sat silently, looking up at the white haired Elder who taught them, as he continued.

"A creature of the North is Moose. Moose is the largest and loudest member of the deer family. He stands on the hilltop bellowing out, 'I am Moose!' You have all heard the mighty cry of the Moose in the wilderness." Each boy could hear that cry in the ear of his mind.

"That statement of Moose is a statement of truth. It is not arrogant. Arrogance is in the South. Arrogance must pass through the West to be softened by Owl into the truth of the North. You see, Moose Medicine is the medicine of Self-Esteem. Moose knows who he is and declares it clearly. In the spirit of Moose, one says, 'This is what I do, and I do it well, because it comes from who I am! I don't do that well, for that is another.' In the spirit of Moose, there is no envy or jealousy. One recognizes one's own well-doing and owns it, and respects and honors the well-doing of others."

"With Moose, one recognizes that by working together in cooperation and synergy, a much greater thing can be accomplished than by each working alone. Moose medicine guides our tribe and is the spirit by which we succeed in surviving and thriving!" They now understood well how each of them must deal with their own arrogance and competitive spirit and learn to

cooperate, even celebrating the learning and accomplishments of each other.

The Elder stood silently for a long time waiting for each boy to ponder the importance of Moose. Then he continued. "Another creature of the North is Buffalo. Buffalo is our way of life. He gives us food and clothing. You have begun to hunt with the men of the tribe, and you know how we follow the great Buffalo herds. When we take a Buffalo, we first pray, thanking Great Spirit for leading us to the herd, and then thanking the great beast for giving its life that the people may live. And nothing of that great beast is wasted. Every part of the animal is used. Every tiny bone and sinew is precious and is utilized. Buffalo Medicine is the medicine of Prayer and Abundance."

This was one of the most important teachings the old man had to give. He measured each word carefully, watching the young men to be sure they understood.

"Buffalo is Abundance because the herds are so vast and the Buffalo provide so much to us. We Pray because of the importance of giving thanks for its life and our sustenance." Again he paused for emphasis, and then continued.

"One of the most important things we learn from Buffalo is the Prayer of Gratitude. Wisdom constantly requires the prayer of gratitude from us. In that spirit, Buffalo teaches us an amazing principle. You learn to forgive because forgiveness removes the burden of sin and trespass. Buffalo teaches us there is a higher principle than forgiveness, one that when fully understood and appreciated, renders forgiveness unnecessary, even irrelevant. It is the Principle of Gratitude!" He looked around as each boy stared in surprise. They had always thought it hard enough to forgive. Now they must also be grateful!

"Yes, Gratitude! It is a North Principle and contemplated too early in the journey, it may appear to be folly, even as it now may appear to you. But here is how it works. In the spirit of Buffalo, one looks back at life, at the times one experienced disrespect and hurt at the hands of another, and at the times one felt betrayed and perpetrated upon, even damaged. At such times, Owl was visiting especially hard."

"Then in the spirit of Buffalo one realizes how much one has learned from each of these experiences; how much stronger, how much greater character, and how much growth has resulted. Had we not had such experiences and sought the growth that came from them, we would have remained as we were. It was those experiences that gave us knowledge of ourselves and growth! In a burst of gratitude, one realizes that these difficulties and perpetrations were not curses, they were blessings!

"That is the great Principle of Gratitude! It brings us not to forgiveness, for we recognize we were truly blessed by our pains and our perpetrators! Indeed, it brings us to gratitude, gratitude for every experience that made us stronger, and brought us higher in the journey of life! We now realize how good life is. We look upward to our Creator with gratitude for the perfect life and perfect life experiences we have been given, for our ultimate growth and learning where only good is the result!"

Now he paused for several moments, looking around the circle of youths. He knew that this was a teaching that would take many years of living, struggle, and experience for his young charges to comprehend. It is truly a North Principle. And he reflected on the long path of growth he had lived before he had become truly grateful for the challenges he had experienced along the way. He could feel the swell of gratitude within him for his own personal path of growth, leading ultimately to Wisdom and to this moment with these young men.

Now he bent down to his bundle and took out one final item. It was a rattle, made from the cloven hoof of an Elk, the two hollow hoof-claw parts filled with small stones and attached firmly to the elk's leg bone. Shaking it vigorously, he spoke. "This rattle comes from Elk. Elk is a prey animal, yet Elk survives its predators not by running faster, but by keeping on running. When mountain lion finally becomes tired and bored from the chase, Elk is still going! Elk Medicine is the medicine of Stamina. While Eagle flies

with us in our journey around the circle to give us courage, Elk runs alongside of us with the encouragement to keep on going. Don't get discouraged. Don't give up. When the journey gets hard and Owl is digging his talons into your spirits and the pain is especially strong, keep going. The North is always ahead!"

"Remember Wolf in the South," he spoke softly. "Again we see balance shown in the circle. The knowledge gained with Wolf in the South must pass through the experiences with Bear, Crow, and Owl in the West before it becomes Wisdom in the North!"

Removing his headband, he shook his white hair briskly, letting it cascade down his shoulders. "The color of the North is white. It is the white of the stars and moon that come out in the night sky at the end of the day cycle. It is the white of the snow that blankets Mother Earth in the winter of the year cycle. It is the color of the White Light that fills the healed soul with the joy of being in the North of the life cycle.

"There remains one final creature you must welcome into your lives. It is Coyote, the Trickster. Coyote has no place in the circle, but rather he wanders with us. Coyote is our guide. You see, Coyote tells us to not take ourselves too seriously as we journey. Coyote says that if we take ourselves and life too seriously, he will come around and bite us in the butt! Now it is important that you think on this. When you are going down the road of life feeling Owl's pain and feeling all pitiful and sorry for yourself, Coyote sinks his teeth deep into one of your butt cheeks. Now you are dragging not only yourself down the road, but also Coyote with his teeth in you. Blood is running down your leg. It is at that moment you need to walk across the road from yourself and look back. You need to see yourself feeling all pitiful and victimized. You need to see yourself feeling all sorry for yourself. Keep looking until you can laugh at this pitiful image of yourself and ask how you allowed the magnificent being you are to devolve into this sorry and pitiful creature. Laugh until you can be grateful to Coyote for sinking his teeth into your butt to get your attention and remind you not to take yourself and your life

so seriously! Remember, you are living a perfect life for your learning and growth!"

With that, the old story teller went back to his pipe and bundle, and knelt down. Silently and respectfully he packed his things up. He ignored the boys. He had finished his work with them. As they saw that he was finished speaking to them, one by one they got up and quietly left the lodge. The old man had given them a map of symbols and medicine metaphors. It was now up to each boy to individually and personally ponder and reflect on the teachings, as each one walked on into manhood and his personal circle of life.

Before the Elder left the lodge, he looked around and thought of all the people who wander aimlessly through the challenges of life, not knowing these kernels of wisdom and pearls of great price. He wished for all people that some guidance like he had given the young men would become available for them. And so this book came into being.

The Principles—

The Principles for satisfying living come in four groups. The first group is the Principles of Growth and Learning. These principles lay out the foundation upon which you must base your life if you really want to grow out of victimhood and experience the Empowered Life. And these principles come in order. You must start with the first principle and progress down the list. If you are not willing to get vulnerable, you are not ready to begin the journey to an empowered life.

The second group of principles relates to decisions you must make to apply the principles in your life. They lay out the four decisions you must make in order to experience an empowered life.

The third group contains three critical decisions you must make if you want to support others to join you on the journey to an empowered life. Here you will see how support requires that you come to grips with your own tendencies to enable victimhood through desiring others to feel good and like you.

The fourth group is The Simple Principles of Empowerment. They are really very simple and there are only five. You will find these five simple principles in every enlightened philosophy. They may be stated in somewhat different forms, but they are universal through all human cultures.

There is one final overarching principle that gives you an important tool for truly empowering your life. I call it The Mirror Principle. Chapter One explains this key principle. If you really *get it,* you will have the best tool available to empower your life, for you will then have the tool that reveals exactly what is driving your life experience, all day, every day. With the powerful Mirror Principle you can *take charge* of everything in your experience of living!

Coyote leads you on to consider these principles.

The Principles of Growth and Learning
(In Order)

If you want to grow, you must be willing to:

1. Get Vulnerable.

Be willing to expose the edges of your life. Accept that it is absolutely OK to be human, OK to be you *including all your strengths and weaknesses*. Be willing that others know both your strengths and weaknesses. Be working toward the ideal that it is OK to be human and that you are comfortable enough with yourself that to be known AS YOU ARE does not threaten you. **Growth Goes Hand In Hand With Risk!**

2. Get Real.

Stop pretending. Get out of denial. Be willing to deal with reality. Seek the truth about yourself, your beliefs and attitudes, your perceptions, your reputation, your circumstances, your relationships, and everything in your life.

3. Get Responsible.

Live from the attitude that everything in your life has resulted from choices you have made, that you are not a victim of anything, that you have within your sphere of control workable solutions to every problem and challenge, and that you are fully accountable for everything you say and do. Eliminate *blame, stories and excuses* from your life.

4. Tell The Truth. (The outward expression of Get Real!)

Always, relentlessly, boldly, courageously, personally, professionally, openly, without exception. Build your reputation on telling the truth— even the microscopic truth.

5. Keep Your Word. (The outward expression of Get Responsible!)

Always, to a fault, without exception, build your reputation on keeping your word.

Applying the Principles of Growth

If you *Really* want to grow and experience empowerment in your life, you must be willing to base your life on these four decisions:

1. Life Is A Choice.

I choose my attitudes and my beliefs, values, expectations, and conclusions about myself and my world. Circumstances in my life come and go. They just ARE. I always choose how I respond to the circumstances that come into my life (have always, will always). I define and give meaning to my life. I am not entitled to anything. The Universe owes me nothing but my place in it.

2. I Own My Entire Life, Period!

My life today is exactly the result of all the choices I have ever made, no more, no less. And I am the *only one* who ever made a choice *in my life*. I am not a victim of anything!

    a. *Blame* is an irrelevant activity. It produces no growth or empowerment.

    b. *Manipulation* and *Justification* arise in my life from the conclusions I made as a child. They accompany blame for circumstances and choices in the past, and lead to no growth, healing, or change in the present.

3. I Live In The Present.

The past is no longer relevant, except for lessons to learn. The past JUST IS! Nothing can ever be done to change it. The present is the ONLY place where I can make new choices that will bring about positive change in my life.

4. My Experience Of Life Is A Mirror Of My Internal State.

Everything that causes my experience of life is filtered through my beliefs, expectations, and conclusions about myself and my world (which *I* either *Decided* or *Bought*!). The world I perceive and experience *is a reflection of my internal state* (no more, no less!). *I Create My Experience* through the decisions and choices I make about how I perceive and deal with the circumstances that come into my life. This has been so from conception and infancy to this very moment!

Issues of Support in
Applying the Principles of Growth

If you *Really* want to support your family, friends, associates, employees, or clients in the process of personal growth and empowerment, you must be willing to come from these decisions:

1. **The *Feels Good Issue***

   Life is not primarily about feeling good. It is primarily about growth. "As your supporter in the process of growth and empowerment, I care more about your personal growth and empowerment than I do about you or me 'feeling good.'"

2. **The *Approval/Acceptance Issue***

   Self-esteem is not determined by acceptance or approval. It is primarily determined by standing for one's inner truth and one's principles. "As your supporter in the process of growth and empowerment, I care more about your personal growth and empowerment than I do about your opinion of me."

3. **The *Enabling Issue***

   Your self-esteem and growth are not supported by my acceptance or tolerance of your self-defeating and addictive behaviors, dysfunctions, or lack of integrity. "As your supporter in the process of growth and empowerment, I hold both you and me fully and personally accountable for living principles that work and for keeping the agreements we have made."

The Simple Principles of Empowered Living

1. Life Is.

People just are. Circumstances just are. Stuff happens. Everything pertaining to whether something is good or bad in your perception is a judgment that you make about it. The things that produce the greatest learning, growth, and character in your life are those that challenge you the most! Why not decide right now that your life is good and be grateful for every challenge and adversity. Look for the learning, growth, and character building in everything you experience.

2. The only moment of importance in life is *Now*.

The past can never be changed. It just is, and will remain so forever, even as you create it moment by moment! The only value of the past is to learn from it. In the past you see the consequences from every choice you made and how you chose to deal with those consequences. Learn what you can from the past and then let it go. The only moment in which you can make a new choice that will affect the future you want is *Now*. Apply what you learn from the past in making those choices!

3. I am absolutely responsible for my entire life, *Period*.

You are the only who ever made a choice in your life. You are the only one who decides how you will respond to every person and circumstance in your life. And your experience of life right now is exactly the consequence of all the choices you ever made. Blame is an irrelevant activity. You are the one who decides what your internal state is and no one else ever forces you to have any particular internal experience. There is no such thing as a victim. There is only the choice to perceive the world through the beliefs of blame and victimhood. No one can offend you or make you angry. Others only behave. You are the one who decides to be offended or get angry! Stuff happens. You decide how you will deal with it!

4. What I have in my life is exactly the result of my <u>priorities</u>.

Your priorities, conscious and subconscious, drive every choice you make. And every choice you make has consequences. What you have in your life right now is exactly the result of all the choices you ever made and the priorities that drove them. Your life is a <u>perfect mirror of your priorities</u>. If you want to see what your priorities are, look in the mirror of what you have in your life and your results. It's that simple.

5. If I keep on doing what I've always done, I keep on getting what I've always got!

This is the Principle of Proactivity! Your life experience will continue exactly as it is until YOU decide to change it. Empowerment is a conscious choice. Experiencing an empowered life is deciding to change the habits of a lifetime <u>and doing it</u>. It's that simple!

The Beginnings of My Journey—

I have lived several decades on the planet, even pursuing a career in life coaching and personal development facilitation, teaching all sorts of wonderful principles to audiences with members who told me their lives had been changed. Ah, the kindness and patience of the Universe. To teach is not necessarily *to get!* **Owl** had to visit *me* for me to really **Get** *how deceived I had been* in my own life, even while I taught great and wonderful principles to others. **Owl** visited me often and, like most of us who are committed to being Right about Reality, I avoided looking honestly at the real deceptions in my own life. It was always more convenient to blame others and to avoid seeing my own patterns. My ex-wife of a 30-year marriage: *If only she. . .then I. . . .*My children: *If only they. . .then I. . . .*My associates and coworkers: *If only they. . .then I. . . .*And on and on—these are common blaming/victim patterns of self-deception and creating illusion to justify my failure to live more truthfully and, therefore, joyfully.

Finally, a loving and kind Universe sent a woman into my life, an emissary of **Owl**. "Hope of Forever Soul Mates" penetrated deeply into my soul and **Owl** finally got my attention. Oh, how I desired to "fix her" (more of: *If only she. . .then I. . . .*)! The pain became so intense that my insistence on being Right finally cracked! (I might add just to acknowledge how OK it is to be human, she also desired to "fix me." Ah, the mirrors of relationship!) The breakthrough came when I was *blessed* with pneumonia. Yes, blessed!

I was so sick I could not get out of bed. I had to spend days alone with myself, thinking my thoughts and feeling my feelings. In that painful and blessed bed of affliction, looking into my own mirror of life, I finally *Got It!*

It never had anything to do with her. I am the one who set up all my beliefs. I am the one who set up all my expectations. I am the one who defined every role in my Reality. I am the one who made every choice pertaining to my life. She innocently walked into *a role* in my Reality, a role *I had defined* by My Beliefs and My Expectations. I never saw her. *I only saw my definition of the role she filled.* She had no way of knowing my definition of that role any more than I had of knowing hers. In fact I didn't even consciously know all of my own role definitions! The sum total of all the beliefs and expectations that defined my Reality existed in my subconscious and only came to the surface *when they were violated or challenged!* And boy did she violate them! (And vice versa.)

It might be useful for you to re-read and ponder the last several underlined sentences. *If you can personally get my realization, it will change your life, especially in your relationships!*

The great realization was that it never had anything to do with her! I could almost hear **Owl** sigh with relief. My pain resulted from the beliefs and expectations *I* had chosen to set up for my reality, and to reduce the pain, *I could either change my beliefs* or *I could change my relationship.* She had actually come to a similar realization and we finally got real with each other. We decided that our perceptions of Reality were different enough that, rather than continue to impose unfair and unrealistic expectations on each other, it would be kinder and wiser to separate, which we did. However our brief journey together was a most incredible gift from the Universe for my personal growth, and, in its pain and challenge, was the real beginning of my personal journey toward Empowerment. Thank you Universe for turning up the screws until *I* finally got the Deception and realized that I was not a victim. Thank you Universe for that precious gift from Owl!

What is your precious gift from **Owl**?

-Notes to Self-

Section Two—
The Healing Process of the Medicine Circle

Chapter 1—The Box: Setting the Stage

Chapter 2—Illumination

Chapter 3—Vulnerability

Chapter 4—Deception

Chapter 5—Unconditional

Chapter 6—The Inner-Directed Life

Chapter 7—Ownership and Self-Esteem

Chapter One—

The Box: Setting the Stage

This book deals with life as it is, but presents its lessons in metaphors. I like the metaphorical symbols of the Native American Medicine Circle and will use its powerful metaphors for most of the Principles and ideas throughout the rest of this book. Before we get to that, there is another very useful metaphor that will assist us to set the stage for how life works and why we experience it the way we do. And so we begin with The Box.

We all live in a box. You, I, your family members, your friends and associates, all of us. We each live in a box, each one of us. Sit back for a moment and picture yourself there in the middle of your box. You don't actually see your box surrounding you, but you can imagine for a moment that it is there. Your entire perception of reality is projected onto the inside of your box. You believe you are looking out onto a world out there, and that you see the reality of that world, but everything you perceive in life, coming into your consciousness through all of your senses, is a *projection on the inside of your box—a projection of what is on the inside of you.*

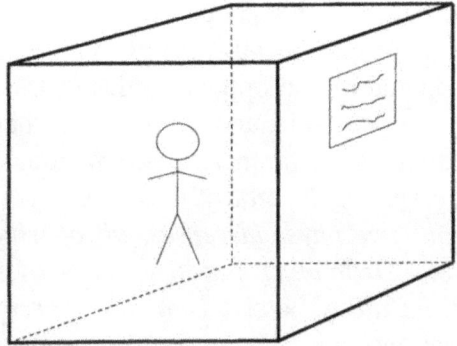

Everything you perceive from all of your senses, sight, hearing, touch, smell, taste, even the stuff that comes to your consciousness from within you, your inner thoughts and ideas, your intuition, it's all there, projected onto the inside of your box. The Box represents the core of your consciousness, the seat of your mind, your conscious awareness, where you perceive reality.

We now deal with **perception of reality** as contrasted with reality itself. Pay attention carefully. None of us knows what is real. Not one of us, no one! *No human being knows what is real.* All any of us know and can deal with in life is our *perception of what is real.* Can you see why this is true? Your experience of life and all the choices you make in life, all you ever have to work with in life is **your perception** *of what is real!*

Our senses are the only means that we have to get information from outside of the core of our consciousness. Our five physical senses and our inner sense, including the thoughts, ideas, inspirations, and intuition that comes to us from inside our minds. *Everything* that comes into our core of consciousness, through every one of our six senses, *is a perception!* Every one of our senses *is a perceptual sense.*

Some pondering may help you better comprehend this truth. Pause now and do some critical thinking about this point. To continue in disbelief of this concept of The Box, i.e., the idea that no one knows what is real because **all** of our senses are perceptual senses, will put you and me on opposite sides of this fundamental point and I want to sit by your side, and be your friend and companion on your journey of emerging awareness. So ponder this point before continuing: *Everything in reality must enter your mind through one or more of your five physical senses, all of which are perceptual senses, and/or your sixth inner intuitive sense of ideas, thoughts, inspiration, and realizations, which is also a perceptual sense. Think about it! All perception is an interpretation.*

You do not know what is real. You only know and experience *what you perceive to be real.* As far as your experience of the world out there *And your experience of yourself in that world*, you only have available to you your five physical senses and your sixth inner sense to give you *your perception of what is real.* I don't question that there is a reality. It exists. I exist. You exist. But (*and ponder this idea for a while too!*) *I* am not present in your reality. I only exist in your reality *as a perception.* Your family, friends, and associates are not present in your reality. They only exist in your reality *as perceptions.* **You** *yourself* (and this is <u>critically important for you to realize</u>; *ponder it too!*), **You** only exist in your own reality *as a perception!*

So the key question is, *what filters reality into your perception of it?*

The filter that renders reality into your perception of it is the total set of beliefs you have. Your beliefs *define the reality you experience*.

R
E
A
L
I
T
Y

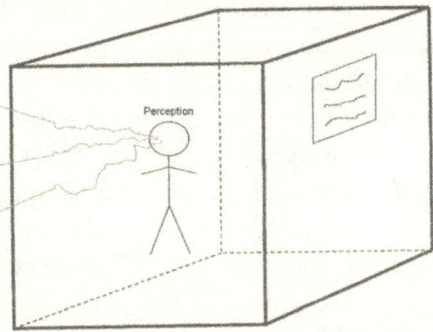

Perception

As you entered mortality at the moment of con-ception and as you developed the capacity to receive inputs from your experience of mortality (beginning after a few weeks of fetal development), you began to form conclusions about your experience. Those early inputs came to you from experiences, and the conclusions you formed about them were not made in your intellectual or Cognitive mind, because that had not yet developed to a sufficient extent. Those conclusions formed in another part of your developing mind called the Affective Mind. Its name is not necessarily important to remember, but it is important to realize that the Affective part of your mind was actively forming conclusions about your reality as you experienced it, even in the womb.

Beginning in the womb, you had very real experiences of the outside world through sounds and movements. You also had very real experiences of your mother's emotions through her emotional chemicals as they passed through the placenta, emotions like anger, passion, fear, excitement, worry. You may not have had any frame of reference for interpreting those experiences, but you had a jolt of the feelings, nonetheless. Your biological inheritance, then, began to give you some experience of the life to come before you had to deal with it directly.

As you emerged into the physical world at birth, you were greeted by an abrupt change in environment: temperature (it got cold!) and light (it got bright!). And many of us were further greeted by the proverbial slap on the butt (it got painful!). Welcome to the real world. Welcome to the experiences of the world!

It might have been nice for you to have found the world to be a pleasant, consistent and predictable place so you, in your Affective Mind, could develop a smooth and reliable strategy for surviving in it. But for most of us the world is not consistent and predictable. Life is not smoothly pleasant. Far from it. Mom and Dad are sometimes gentle and loving. Sometimes they fight with each other. Mom is sometimes totally loving and dedicated to you. Sometimes you are an inconvenience to her. Sometimes your needs are met quickly, sometimes slowly or not at all. Some of the people you might expect you could trust and count on were struggling with dysfunction, addictions, emotional and mental illness, etc. They did not always treat you respectfully or with love and kindness. Trust may well have become an issue for you. The following points apply to all human beings as they enter mortality.

In the world of the infant, there is only one being: *Self.* Differentiation comes slowly. It takes time to realize that you are not the whole world. Infant needs such as hunger, dirty diapers, discomfort, etc., are expressed through crying. They are met by something being placed in the baby's mouth, the baby's bottom being wiped and a clean diaper installed, or the baby's discomfort being somehow removed. To the infant, the needs are simply met. It takes time to realize that there are actually other human beings who take care of these things, and even more time to identify those human beings with titles like Mom and Dad, siblings, etc.

Since, in your world as an infant there was only that one being, namely **You**, your conclusions as an infant were focused on *you*; everything was about *you*. Pain and inconsistency in that infantile state lead to conclusions of doubt and uncertainty about *you*. It is a fairly mature and high order of development to realize that something *out there* is what is bad or to be avoided. Faced with pain and discomfort, the baby's conclusion is focused on self, that **I'm Not OK**, that there is something wrong **With Me**. For most of us, this is the *foundational belief.* Once that foundational belief is in place, the rest of life becomes filling in the details. What is it that is wrong with me? How am I not OK? Since the foundational belief is that "I'm not OK," or

"There is something wrong with me," all of our failures and mistakes in life are then filtered and interpreted through the lens of that belief.

Life becomes a self-fulfilling prophesy. I believe I am not OK, so I see my failures and mistakes as *ongoing evidence* of the truth of my belief! I continue to perceive myself through the filter of my belief. There is something wrong with me, therefore I can't....There is something wrong with me, therefore I don't deserve....There is something wrong with me, therefore I'm not lovable. There is something wrong with me, therefore I don't control my own experience; something out there is doing it to me; I am a victim....

To the newly arrived human infant, there are four fundamental questions necessary for survival in life that must be answered fairly quickly in order to form a strategy for relating and surviving. I call these the Survival Questions. Most organisms answer their survival questions through hard genetic wiring, by instinct. But human infants have to answer them through experience. Human young spend years with their parents learning how to be human beings. How you answered them as an infant is foundational to your Belief System, built directly on the foundation of your fundamental conclusion to the question, *How OK am I?*

The Four Fundamental Survival Questions

1. **How capable am I? (the ability question)**
2. **How much do I matter, how worthy, how deserving? (the self-worth question)**
3. **How lovable am I? (the relationship question, with self and others)**
4. **How much control do I have over my own experience of living? (the victim question)**

Most of us seem to have concluded the answers to these questions with doubt or actually in the negative. Check it out. How many times just in the last few days have you had the thoughts pass through your mind, or the words actually come out of your mouth, "I can't do that!" "I don't deserve that!" "I'm not lovable!" "You offend me. You make me mad!" Start paying attention to your inner self-talk, to your internal filter. Your filter takes circumstances that show up in your life and renders them into conclusions about you, as simple circumstances are filtered through your beliefs. You may discover that your filter renders many of these into *self-defeating conclusions about you!*

You see, all the conclusions you formed about the world, and about you in that world, from infancy on (and mostly in the early years of your life), became your *beliefs about reality.* And when you began to develop language, when your symbolically operating Cognitive Mind began to emerge as your primary interface with your world, your experientially driven Affective Mind dropped out of sight, *into your subconscious.* It became your Belief System, *your internal and subconscious definition of reality, your filter of perception, for the rest of your life.* Your subconscious Belief System *Is* your personal and unique definition of reality. Your subconscious Belief System *Is* the filter through which whatever is real out there (and within you and about you) is filtered into your personal and unique *perception* of it. It is the filter of The Box, within which you will perceive reality for your entire mortal life.

If you haven't had a significant enough experience with something to have formed a meaningful conclusion about it, you won't have a belief about it in your Belief System. And if you don't believe it, *you won't perceive it.* It won't exist for you in your perceived experience of reality.

Check it out. I'm sure you have had the experience of encountering a new word, reading it or hearing it for the first time. Perhaps you even looked it up in a dictionary or made some other effort to learn what it means. Once you have that word defined in your experience, you suddenly find that word again and again. It was always there. You just never perceived it because you did not have any experience of it nor conclusion about it in your Belief System. Once you had an experience of it and put it into your Belief System, you were able to perceive it in your reality, and there it was, over and over.

This leads us to the final overarching principle, **The Mirror Principle**. When you realize that you live in a box and that you don't know what is real, you only know what you *perceive to be real*, and that you have a filter that renders reality into your perception of it, you gain an important tool for personal growth! You also then realize that what you perceive *Is A Mirror* *of your inner conclusions, beliefs, and priorities.* Your perception is an amazing mirror of your Belief System! You perceive what you believe. I cannot stress enough how important the Mirror Principle is for an empowered person. Life's circumstances may indeed contain things that "just happen." But *your experience of life,* how you feel about and deal with life and its circumstances, is a perfect mirror that reflects back to you the conclusions, beliefs, and priorities that drive your choices and your responses. This is another time to pause and ponder! You are the creator of your life experience.

Now back to the question of Who Is Right? Think back to a recent conflict you had with someone. There was some situation or set of circumstances or idea that was perceived differently between you and that other person or group. Both of you, or all of you, were filtering the subject of your disagreement through your respective filters. Those filters were composed of the accumulated experiences and conclusions made during the lifetimes of everyone involved. Reality was filtered through two or more Belief Systems and rendered into two or more different (and unique) perceptions: *filtered into different and unique perceptions!*

So Who Is Right?

Does *your* perception, based on *your* life experiences and conclusions since you were an infant, *and founded on your infantile conclusions,* have any more inherent validity than anyone else's perception based on their life experiences and conclusions since they were an infant, *and founded on their infantile conclusions?* It is a pretty arrogant statement to say *I am right in my perception and you are wrong in your perception!* But we make that statement all the time to others in our life! I cannot possibly know all the experiences and internal conclusions that have become your Belief System and filter your perception any more than you can know all of mine. Each of us is filtering the same reality through our individual filters into our unique and personal perception of it.

The issue, then, is *Never* Who Is Right? The issue is *always* one of staying in communication, back and forth, expressing and listening, sharing perceptions and experiences, until an outcome evolves with which both or all can be satisfied! Read this again! This is a critical empowerment skill, staying in communication until an outcome evolves with which both or all can be satisfied. I call such an outcome *Consensus*! And with consensus, both, or all, buy into the outcome, each for his or her own reasons. We don't have to agree on the reasons. We just have to find personal reasons to buy into the outcome!

The Native Americans taught me a simple tradition to avoid arguments over who is right and derive a satisfactory outcome. I refer to it as the "Talking Feather." It may involve a feather, a stick, a stone, car keys, or anything available, which is passed around the circle. Here is how it works. The group sits in a circle and agrees on the item, and then to a simple set of ground rules. A version of this strategy could be useful in a family, neighborhood, business, or any organization to help resolve or avoid problems.

The Talking Feather Ground Rules

1. Everyone agrees to these ground rules, and to stay with this process until an outcome has evolved with which all can be satisfied.
2. The item starts anywhere. Once underway, the circle has no head or leader.
3. The item passes sunwise (clockwise) around the circle from person to person.
4. As the item passes around the circle, the one holding it at a time has the floor and may speak, and then passes it on to the next person when finished speaking.
5. No one else may speak until the item comes around to him or her.
6. As each person, in turn, receives the item, he/she may speak, or pass it on.
7. All participants commit to listen quietly and respectfully to each person, and to all points of view as they are expressed. No one may speak until he/she has the item.

8. All participants agree that the circle will remain, and the item continue to pass around, until an outcome evolves with which everyone finds satisfaction.
9. If this requires breaks for toilet, eating, or sleeping, so be it. Such breaks are taken.
10. Only when an outcome has evolved with which *everyone* finds satisfaction (which I define as *consensus*), is the circle dissolved, and the outcome implemented. This may require considerable time, hours, days, weeks, to which all have agreed.

This is a gift from our native brothers and sisters that can be used by any couple, any group, any work team, any neighborhood, any gang, any tribe that wants to avoid the destructive effects of discord and fighting over who is right. Peace may be difficult to achieve but it is *Not Impossible*!

There is another aspect of the mirror that is critical to the empowered individual in relationship. Since my perception of reality is what I perceive, projected on the inside of my box, I never really perceive you. I only perceive *my perception of you*. Therefore in our interactions with others, statements that contain the word "you" should be used very carefully. I can talk about *my* experience of you, *my* perception of you, *my* feelings about or judgments of you, *my* attitudes toward you, etc., but I can never talk about *YOU*. I don't know you, or your motives, or your feelings, or anything except *My Perception* of any of these things regarding you. Any comments I might make about you are really more about *Me* and the filters that render you into *my perception of you*, than they are about you. This is a very good thing to keep in mind as you explore the possibilities of empowered relationship!

How we define ourself *to our self* is a final important concept to introduce as we prepare for the journey of empowerment. It derives from the same filter that creates our box. It has to do with how we define ourselves internally, how we define our very identity, how we are fundamentally wired inside to deal with life. It is also derived from the foundational part of our Belief System. To grasp this concept I introduce three words:

Be—Do—Have

These three words form another mirror *by the way they are arranged,* and you may be able to see yourself in this mirror. It is an important mirror for those who are on the empowerment journey and mirrors how one validates self.

Most people in the world are wired HAVE—DO—BE. These people focus on having things, having money, having titles, having approval and admiration for their possessions. Their very identity is tied up with what they possess, the house, the neighborhood, the car, the boat, the job title, the corner office, the accolades. If they were to lose the job, or the house, or the title, etc., they lose their very self-identity and validation, and the foundation of their lives is shaken. Their lives are wired around the idea, "If I *have* these things, then I can *do* such and such, and then I will *be* happy." Happiness is an external pursuit of possession and attainment.

Many other people are wired around the pattern of DO—HAVE—BE. These people focus on doing things, doing good, doing fun, performing well, following orders, or obeying commandments. Their very identity is all tied up with doing activities, gaining approval or acceptance for what they do, for accomplishing things, or for performing. Star athletes might lose their identity if they were injured and could not play. Some religious folks might work hard to earn the approval of God or others through doing good works. Performing musicians or actors might lose their identity if they lost their physical appearance or their capacity to sing or play. These examples represent lives built around the idea, "If I *do* these things, then I can *have* approval, then I will *be* happy, approved, worthy, loved, saved, etc."

Conversely, the Empowered are wired around BE—DO—HAVE. These people accept themselves as validated *by simply existing.* They are primarily concerned with discovering more of who they are, starting from the realization that "I AM OK!" and continuing their journey as primarily one of learning more about the qualities of being that exist within themselves. As they discover more and more of their magnificence as human *beings,* their focus is on developing the inner qualities they possess and manifesting them in their lives. They derive satisfaction from growth and learning because it reflects an increasing magnificence of being. Of course, the more they know about who they are, the more they can express that knowing in terms of accomplishment and achievement. Their lives are wired around the idea, "This is *who I am*; what I *do* flows as a natural extension of who I am; and I *have* the results *and accompanying joy* as a natural outcome." This kind of life is authentic. You are at choice.

I have a hero who exemplifies **BE—DO—HAVE** for me. This hero is Stephen Hawking, a brilliant cosmologist and theoretical physicist. Hawking has been called a modern Einstein and creates theories about the birth and death of the universe, working them out with complex mathematics. He retired not long ago as a full professor at Cambridge University having occupied the faculty chair formerly held by Isaac Newton in the 1600s. He is close to my age now, and, as a young man, was diagnosed with amyotrophic lateral sclerosis, commonly called Lou Gehrig's Disease. Progressively over his life, he lost the capacity to control and move his muscles, even losing his ability to speak. Eventually he became confined to a wheelchair from which he continues to perform his work.

As he progressively lost his ability to "do" with his body, he never lost his mental capacity. His mind remained sharp and fully capable. He continued to lecture at Cambridge, and write and publish books in which he explained his ideas with a sense of humor and in language understandable to the general public. One of his books, *A Brief History of Time,* has a wide distribution to the general public. Perhaps you would enjoy reading it.

Instead of living in self-pity, Hawking kept ahead of his disease by inventing ways to communicate his ideas, even though he could not communicate with his voice. He communicated his mind by employing a few functional facial muscles with which he activated his computer. I have heard him speak to a large crowd in a huge event center using his voice synthesizer. His sense of humor is obvious. He does not live in self-pity for that which he does not *have* but continues to give his gift to the world because of who he *is*. He *Is* a scientist and mathematician. His *Being* drives his passion for finding ways to keep *Doing*. And through his results he *Has* the recognition and appreciation of the world who knows him. I recommend you look his name up and read about him, and read some of his work.

In that same sense, *I Am* a teacher and facilitator. When I began my professional work some decades ago, fresh out of graduate school with a Ph.D. in a scientific field, I was focused on "doing" my science. It took me a dozen years to realize I did not find joy in *doing* my science. *I Was Not* a scientist. I am a bright guy who could *Do* science. I enjoyed *having* the knowledge of my science but not *doing* the work of my science because my *having* and my *doing* were not consistent with my *being*. At my "midlife crisis" I began a journey to find out who *I Am*. It did not take long to begin to see hints, and I followed those hints into opportunities where the answer became clear. *I Am* a teacher and facilitator.

There are some who *do* facilitation, perhaps very well. *I Am* a facilitator. That has an interesting downside. Because *I Am* a facilitator, that expression of myself flows out of me naturally and spontaneously. Not everyone with whom I engage wants a facilitator. But they may get one, uninvited, unless I exercise some recognition of my natural tendency and express myself in other more appropriate ways consistent with the moment. In my journey of discovery, it has been important to develop options of expression that are appropriate to many kinds of relationships. In discovering who you are, it is a good idea to become acquainted with yourself in multiple dimensions, and create good options for self-expression that are appropriate to interactions in each of them. Keep looking in the mirror!

Perception, vs. Reality. Be, Do, Have. Accepting and realizing The Box within which you, I, and each of us lives and within which we perceive our reality. This is a good place to begin our journey to empowerment.

Perhaps you might find it useful to take a moment to think about some conflicts you have had that resulted in people having less than satisfactory feelings. Consider how different perceptions of circumstances or outcomes were involved. Consider how communications were cut off or stifled by participants who insisted on Being Right. Consider how the outcome could have been made more positive or satisfying to everyone involved. Write down observations and realizations about yourself that you can apply to such conversations in the future to achieve more satisfying results. And write down your insights on how you are wired with respect to **Be—Do—Have**. What is the order of the words in *your* self-definition? What have you noticed so far about who you are? What options have you found to express your being in your own multiple dimensions? As you get clear on your own wiring, consider who you relate to and why you form relationships with and/or judgments about them.

-Notes to Self-

Chapter Two—

Illumination

Most of us live unexamined lives. We are so busy living we don't pause to notice the patterns: patterns of choices, patterns of similar or ongoing results, patterns of familiar circumstances, patterns of familiar relationships, those feelings of "this has happened before." The process of healing and transformation begins when some circumstance or situation becomes so intense or painful that it gets our attention. The Sun rises on our opportunities to take on our lives and deal with the life issue triggered by the circumstance and the pain associated with it. The pain illuminates the issue so that we may be prompted to deal with it. It is **Owl** visiting us from the West, the place of maturity, but the process begins in the East.

Why are you reading this book right now? What prompted you to pick it up? What is going on in your life right now that gets your attention? What patterns do you notice? Where do you feel victimized, betrayed, or attacked? What do you wish were different? Where do you feel that *if only* your spouse, boss, child, friend, or circumstance were different, then you could be happy?

If only. . . .

Does it hurt bad enough yet? Come on now, be courageous with **Eagle**. Take an honest look. If there is any little hint in your mind or your feelings that *if only something out there were different,* **then** *you could be happy, And* you are motivated to keep reading, perhaps you have stumbled onto the beginning point for your journey to Empowerment! Now, thank Owl for getting your attention and embrace **Eagle** as the bringer of the Message of Spirit, take courage, and let's embark on the journey.

For many of us, the journey begins with the realization that *we set up our own life* in infancy and early childhood through a series of unconscious conclusions we drew about Reality and ourselves in

Reality. [In Chapters 1 and 14, I discuss in detail what I mean by Reality. For now, Reality for any individual is what that individual perceives. Reality is defined *by the individual* in terms of what he or she *believes* Reality to be! These are the conclusions referred to here.]. These conclusions about Reality were made before we had cognitive brain functions to analyze things and draw resourceful and logical conclusions. These conclusions were made in a part of our psyche where we learn from our experiences. This is what I call the Affective Mind. This part does not reside in our thinking mind (the Cognitive Mind, which was not yet developed). However, these conclusions became the foundation on which we built the rest of our life. As Cognition became our conscious interaction with our world, the Affective conclusions dropped out of sight into our subconscious, *where they still reside* as our Belief System. Remember that these conclusions *determine our Perception of Reality* and form *the filter* through which we perceive and give meaning to everything in life: our perceptual box. Some authors refer to these conclusions, or Belief System, as our "Paradigm." Your Paradigm *Is* your Reality, as you perceive it. And *you* concluded it from your early experiences; our foundational beliefs and core perceptions are usually formed by age three. Here is a summary of the process.

How I Set Up My Life and Paradigm

1. **The Infant/Child's Experiential Discovery:** Life doesn't make sense (because I experience it as inconsistent, painful, unfair). Sometimes my parents fight, my pet dies, my grandpa goes away, my toy is gone, sometimes Mommy is loving and sometimes she is angry, etc.
2. **Resulting Belief About Myself:** I get it! I'm not OK! There is something wrong with me! *(To the child this conclusion explains the inconsistency and unfairness and brings sense to life! It forms the basis for the Reality each of us constructs.)*
3. **Evidence for Correctness of Belief:** In my interpretation of life, my ongoing experiences, results, and behaviors are *always* consistent with this fundamental conclusion and the beliefs that are derived from it: my incapability, my unworthiness, my

unlovability, and my victimhood *(because they are all perceived through the filter of these beliefs!)*.

4. **Standard of Comparison:** Seen through this filter, Mom's and Dad's expectations of me *always verify* that I am right about myself. I *especially* notice when I don't live up to their expectations, providing *ongoing, even lifelong* verification of my beliefs about myself. My perceptions of Mom's and Dad's expectations and judgments are constantly and subconsciously with me, driving my experience of myself and life throughout my life. Being right means pleasing or agreeing with them.

5. **Continuing Conclusion:** See, I'm Right! My life proves it! The adults in my life are pleased with me or agree with my beliefs.

6. **Life Results:** *Always consistent with my fundamental beliefs* and I always get to *Be Right* about my childhood conclusions about myself and my Reality, even to the present moment *(because my results, and my perceptions of myself, are always filtered through my beliefs and expectations! See, my life and results prove I'm Right!)*.

7. **Solution:** Do nothing and continue to Be Right, **OR** *admit that I may Be Wrong about my conclusions of who I am and what is possible for me,* and address my core beliefs and conclusions about myself and my Reality. Maybe *I am actually OK, even magnificent,* with infinite potential waiting to be unleashed! Maybe I really can handle my life and actually create a wonderful and joyful experience of living!

The words "right" and "wrong" as I am using them are judgments one may make as to whether a belief, or a set of beliefs, leads to an empowering experience of life. The point here is not to engage in a "right/wrong" game about life. I maintain that one is always "right" about what one perceives, because it *is* what one perceives. But, the meaning, the interpretation, the application, the learning from, the implications, and the choices based upon any perception may be shifted to be more consistent with present time, adult perceptions and empowerment. Empowerment begins with the realization that my Belief System is not rigid, but is flexible.

The question then is not *Is It Right?* but rather **Does It Work?** I can change my perception! And I am then "right" again in my new and more empowered perception. Let my use of the word "wrong" be a challenge and an invitation to question and examine the present-time workability of the conclusions and beliefs that drive your results, and not a judgment of any particular set of conclusions and beliefs.

People search for meaning in life. Many people interpret life as though they were some kind of pawns in some grand universal scheme of things with their lives determined by forces outside of themselves. What if life *Just Is*? What if *existence* is the Great Gift the Universe bestows on us? What if beyond existing, *everything else is up to me?* What if we arrive in mortality with our individual genetic package, into a particular set of family circumstances, and then have a completely blank slate before us? What if whatever is put on that slate, including how we deal with our genetic package and our family circumstances is a choice we can make? What if we were to hold the circumstantial stuff associated with our DNA, and the physical, mental, emotional stuff we possess personally, and the stuff that pertains to family and circumstances that surround us when we arrive, all in this same context that *we are not victims of it, but can exercise choice to transcend it.*

The stuff we arrive with is the "hand of cards" we are dealt in the game of life. Beyond that, what if it is completely up to us to take whatever cards we drew and make of it what we will? What if our upbringing and all the stuff we experienced as children is just part of the circumstantial package in the cards we drew in the game of life? What if all the mistakes our parents made, our teachers made, and any of those who perpetrated upon us made, are just part of that circumstantial package? What if *every hand* can be played as a _winning hand_? What if, at any moment of *NOW*, we could **just accept** our particular set of past circumstances, notice the conclusions we drew back then about ourselves and reality, and *decide _in the present moment_* to move on to whatever we want in our future? What if living an Empowered Life only requires making such a simple decision in the present moment? Just make a new choice! A choice to learn from the past, let go of the past, and move on toward the future we want! I believe it is that simple! That doesn't mean it is easy. ***But it is simple***!

Our experience of life is basically a habit; all patterns are habits or addictions. We persist in the habit of being right about our childhood conclusions, for instance. We interact in habitual patterns with our circumstances. We make habitual choices in how we deal with life. Breaking habits is not necessarily easy. But it is simple! **Growth requires constant and *conscious* substitution of the desired new pattern in place of the old whenever the old shows up. It requires that we *consciously* put the adult in charge whenever the habits and patterns of the child show up. It requires that we put our *conscious mind* in control of our *subconscious* tendencies and habits. It requires commitment! We must *grow up* and be *conscious adults*!**

A wonderful movie illustrates this. In "A Beautiful Mind," John Nash, a genius mathematician and eventual Nobel Prize winner, battles with schizophrenia. The movie is based on John Nash's actual life. The turning point in the movie comes when he decides he can solve the problem in his own mind rather than be returned to the hospital for more drug and shock treatment. In the movie, he is never completely without his illusions, but he recognizes them for what they are and *consciously chooses* to ignore them. He *decides* to put his rational mind in charge of his life and commits himself to move on to what he wants.

This is the key to empowerment for any life, even yours!

The First Realization of the Empowered Life is to simply and absolutely take responsibility for it. You journey to the core of your soul and make *these critical decisions:* **I have only *one* life to live. *I* am absolutely responsible for my life, without exception. *I* am the *only one* who lives my life and the only one who ever makes a choice *in my life*. I have made *every choice* pertaining to my experience of life from conception to the present moment. *I* either made the choice myself or *I chose to accept* choices made by others. Circumstances come into my life. *I* am absolutely responsible for how *I* interpret them and how *I* deal with them. *I am not a victim of anything!***

This principle applies to everything in life. Another incredible example of how this principle empowers life is found in the book, *Man's Search for Meaning*, by Viktor Frankl. I strongly recommend you read this transformational book!

Viktor Frankl was a Jewish psychiatrist who survived Auschwitz. I have no personal frame of reference to comprehend what he experienced there. The closest I have come is perhaps through a movie like "Schindler's List," or by visiting the Holocaust Museum in Washington, D.C. Frankl lived it, and at Auschwitz discovered what he considered to be the ultimate human freedom.

Frankl defined freedom as having *choice* among options, and even in the hell of Auschwitz, he discovered that he had a place within himself that they could not control, where he had choice. He discovered that in that inner place, they could not *force him* to hate them. He had options! In this discovery he became a *free man! He could choose his response* even to the unspeakable circumstances surrounding him; this was his last, ultimate, and irrevocable freedom. He also recognized this in others around him who, in the midst of degradation, could choose to share a crumb of bread, to tell a story, to lift another with an act of kindness.

As Viktor Frankl shared with us in his remarkable book, there exists in the human spirit the capacity to accept circumstances as they are, and to choose a different, perhaps higher, helpful, or hopeful response. His circumstances did not change. *But his experience of living his life within them changed.* He gave himself options for feeling and experiencing! For every human being there exists *OPTIONS*. It is the recognition of Options that gives us power and freedom! Viktor Frankl is a hero of mine. If Viktor Frankl could choose his response to *that* set of circumstances, surely *I* can choose my response to any set of circumstances *I* might encounter in *my life!* How about you?

Life attitude is like a pendulum. Most people live with the pendulum swung to the side of being victimized by people and circumstances. Blame is a word often used when the pendulum is swung to that side. Working toward Empowerment and with a new attitude of Being Totally Responsible for one's life, one might swing the pendulum to the other extreme, to the belief that one *creates* all the unfortunate stuff that comes into one's life. Note that this shifts victimhood from being a victim of outside circumstances to being a victim of *one's own unconscious choices or unexamined expectations!* This is equally disempowering! Do you see that tendency in yourself?

The empowering attitude lies at equilibrium. One accepts that in life, a person may not always consciously choose their circumstances; however, they can always choose their response to them. Viktor Frankl certainly did not choose nor create his circumstance of being shipped in a cattle car to Auschwitz. But he did choose to accept that which he could not control (his circumstances; no option there) and choose to control that which he could (his attitude and his response; full of options). He gives us an incredible example of the human capacity for Empowerment!

Remember the Serenity Prayer:

God grant me
The Serenity to accept the things I cannot change,
The Courage to change the things I can, and
The Wisdom to know the difference.

-Notes to Self-

Chapter Three—

Vulnerability

We all have a wall deep within us, a wall we have built, behind which we hide all that stuff we believe condemns us. I call this hiding place within The Wall of Shame and Guilt. It is the inner wall we use to hide the stuff we dare not reveal. No one gets to look back there; we do not like looking there. It hides all the stuff about ourselves that we will not accept or admit, and may not even be conscious of. It divides our inner shame and our public denial from the image by which we want to be seen.

That wall is a personal monument to our human tendency for **Arrogance**!

Who in the Universe said I had to be Superhuman or that it was not OK for me to have weaknesses or make mistakes? Who said that it was not OK to be me as I am, or that I had to be born a "perfect" child and live as a "perfect" adult according to some standard? Who decided that to screw up and make a mess meant that I should be shamed and my terrible misdeeds recorded forever in some book of sins written in the stones of the Universe? Who decided that I would thereafter be held accountable for every mess in my life and incur the condemnation not only of other, more perfect humans, but also the condemnation of God? Who decided that because I am human and I made messes that were recorded somewhere, I had to punish myself to wash away my shame and guilt, so that I could have an acceptable place in the Universe? How good do I have to be to be good enough?

Who said it? *I said it!*

Perhaps it is my futile attempt to live up to the image I believe my Mom or Dad wanted me to be. Or the ideal image some other authority figure in my life set for me. Perhaps it is the comparison I draw between myself and the picture I believe I am expected to live up to according to some standard written in sacred writ or set by my culture, self, family, or society. Who gets to decide for me how I am to be?

Some might see in my declaration a challenge to religious doctrine. I do not intend it to be such. I simply believe in a Creator who is more concerned with my growth and learning than with judging me. I believe in a Creator who sent me here *to learn from my experiences and my mistakes*. I believe in a Creator who does not hold my mistakes against me and who actually rejoices with me when I make mistakes, *especially when I am motivated to learn from them*. I believe in a Creator who sent us forth into life with great opportunities for discovering who we are. I believe in a Creator who created us in Their image (male and female; which many of the Native Americans see as Father Sky and Mother Earth), *imbued with divine magnificence*. There is a familiar song taught to children of many faiths: *I am a Child of God.* I believe it is important for each person to ponder that song title. That is a *State of Being.* I *AM* a child of God. Nothing I ever *DO* in my life will change that fundamental reality of *who I am!* Ponder this for a while.

Whether you believe in a Creator or not, you only have to look around you to see the incredible evidence of what the human mind and spirit can accomplish! Human beings are magnificent bundles of incredible potential! Each one of us is entitled to enormous Respect and Admiration from both self and others, no matter what one's personal or family circumstances, simply for *being human*. Each one of us is a Human Being and possesses the DNA and qualities of human magnificence! To look at the newborn infant is to see an amazing creation of beauty with Magnificent Potential, however that potential expresses itself, from autism to genius, from physical or mental disability to every form of ability and accomplishment, in every expression of the human experience, in every facet of interaction with the rest of us, in all its remarkable diversity of culture and practice. The Human Being is worthy of respect and encouragement. You are a Human Being. Welcome to the human race!

If we are children of God, as C.S. Lewis wrote, you never met a mere mortal. In looking to a Creator for your existence, you acknowledge that *the DNA of Godhood flows in your spiritual veins*. Looking at yourself from *any* perspective of humanhood, you must acknowledge *that the DNA of magnificence lies in every cell of your being.* Looking at yourself from that perspective, for you to focus solely on your mistakes instead of your magnificence *Is Blasphemy* in my opinion! In that focus, you make your worth about your *doing* and not about your fundamental *being*.

All that stuff behind your Wall of Shame and Guilt is a burden you carry. It is the baggage of your past. Because of it, and aided by the judgments and condemnations of your righteous and well-meaning colleagues, your conclusion "I'm not OK!" is continually reinforced that there is something wrong with you. Here is where **Porcupine** joins our journey.

Porcupine invites you to *take a risk and reveal* what is behind that wall. Oh, the shame! Oh, the guilt! Oh, the fear of rejection, unworthiness, and judgment! You shrink back in embarrassment and anxiety. But **Porcupine** continues to encourage you. With **Eagle's** courage you decide to take a risk, and in a safe setting with a trusted friend, you allow a peek behind the Wall. I strongly invite you to take this risk! Find such a friend and go together on a journey with **Porcupine**! Share deeply. Don't hide anything. Open up that wall completely. Where the shamed child fears and hides, let the adult boldly reveal and proclaim.

What a surprise? You are not condemned! Instead, you see on the face of the other compassion and acceptance. You listen as he or she opens their wall. You don't feel judgment or condemnation within you for their stuff, only compassion and acceptance. Together you share a profound compassion and love, born in mutual vulnerability and mutual recognition of the common human experience. Porcupine asks, if you don't condemn each other, why then *do you condemn yourself?*

The Vulnerability of **Porcupine** is not to bring shame and condemnation upon you, but rather to allow you to experience that it is OK to be human, OK to be you. There is nothing wrong with you! You are a perfectly normal human being with strengths *and* weaknesses, like all other human beings. Your strengths are your opportunities to share of yourself. Your weaknesses are your opportunities to learn and grow. Perhaps your weaknesses can even be turned into strengths as you accept them and work on them. Welcome to the Human Race. *Welcome home!*

What if you do feel a bit of judgment or disapproval about what the other person reveals? Do you then beat on yourself for your judgment, or beat on your friend for his or her humanity? What if you detect a bit of negative reaction in the other as you open up your wall and share your own stuff? Do you then shrink back into rightness that you are really not OK after all? The whole journey with **Porcupine** is a journey of patience with yourself. Have faith, both in yourself and in the journey. Just open up to the possibility that below the layers of self-doubt and self-judgment lies a core of beauty and magnificence that will be fully revealed in the course of your journey. Remember the common human DNA that lies at the core of every cell in your body. Remember, who in the Universe said you had to be Superhuman? <u>You did!</u> *You are the one who decided that!* Did you get that? *You Are The One Who Decided You Had To Be Superhuman, Without Weaknesses!* Another option is to conclude it is super to be human, *super to be you!*

Ah, Life! We are here to make messes and to learn to clean them up. I learned this from a fellow facilitator named Gary Acevedo from Salt Lake City. In fact, he says that we are "Mess Making Machines." I wore that, unashamedly, on a nametag once as a volunteer staff member in one of his programs. And I know that I am not finished with making messes in my life. The Empowered Life accepts that every result in every moment provides an opportunity to learn something, even the messes. No mess is a condemnation, it is only an opportunity to learn something and clean up the mess, if possible. Let this become a personal mantra!

Some messes are so big that we can't clean them up. As the arrow of time moves forward, we can't change them. We can only look back on those and learn what we can, do what we can to clean them up, take care of the consequences that we can, *and move on.* The Empowered Life **does not** carry messes as burdens of shame and guilt. **Porcupine** says take them out from behind the Wall and reveal them, learn from them, clean up what you can, *and move on.* Get Vulnerable. For in vulnerability lies the only hope of release. Reveal them and let them go.

The Native Americans have a ceremony called the *Sweat Lodge.* The Sweat Lodge is a representation of the Womb of Mother Earth, the womb of creation. A dome shaped framework, usually of willows, is covered with skins or canvas so that when the door is dropped down over the low entrance, it is completely enclosed and dark inside. Participants crawl in through the door and sit in a circle around the central pit. Stones heated red hot in a fire outside are brought in and placed in the pit, the door is closed, and water is poured onto the hot stones making hot steam. It is a spiritual ceremony of purification and cleansing. I find in that remarkable ceremony a perfect expression of this principle. Get vulnerable. Crawl into the womb. Sweat it out in the heat and the dark. Let it go. Emerge from the womb reborn, cleansed of the baggage of the past, and focused forward toward the vision of what you want in your life.

We can metaphorically go into the womb (and early childhood) where this stuff had its beginnings, by becoming *conscious adults,* and by recognizing that it is only in *our beliefs* of weakness and inferiority that we are not OK in some dimensions of self and that *We* are the ones who created those beliefs! We can consciously replace those subconscious habits of believing with new positive ones. We can consciously substitute positive attitudes of strength and worth for self-limiting ones. It will *feel* unfamiliar and unreal. Let's not be distracted by those unfamiliar feelings! Be committed and persistent in that substitution process. We are the ones who created the beliefs and attitudes that hold us back. Why not create others that drive us forward? Here is where we may need the persistence and patience of **Elk** to not be distracted and discouraged by feelings! Hang in there!

Perhaps it might be useful for you to list below some of the stuff hidden behind your own Wall of Shame and Guilt. As you list things, notice your feelings. What are you *Not* listing because "what if someone should happen to pick up this page and read it?" What things bring up a particularly sharp feeling of shame and regret? Vulnerability with respect to this stuff is your personal key to freedom and self-acceptance! Make a list of possible candidates for that safe person with whom you can have your **Porcupine** conversation. Write down your commitment to have that conversation.

-Notes to Self-

Chapter Four—

Deception

In Chapter Two, I presented a series of steps on how you set up your life to be a disempowered victim. As a new infant human being, you concluded there was something wrong with you. That was the fundamental conclusion to bring sense to your world. That conclusion might have been reasonable from the point of view of the infant, but it formed the basic foundation for your entire Belief System, your Perception of Reality, and charted the course of your life experiences, continuing to the present. The rest of your life has been filling in the details of exactly what is wrong with you. Filtered through that foundational conclusion into your ongoing perception of yourself, life experience and results provided continual evidence that led to these self-defeating conclusions and beliefs, the answers to the four basic survival questions:

I'm not capable.
I'm not lovable.
I'm not worthy.
I'm a victim.

These beliefs take the form of mind chatter and spoken statements like, "I can't do that," "I don't deserve this," "You make me mad!" They show up in our relationships, in the people we believe we deserve to be with and comfortably hang around, in how we relate to those we choose to have in our life. They show up in the jobs we take, the education we gain, the house and neighborhood in which we are comfortable to live. They show up in what we have in our wallets and bank accounts. They show up in the stories we tell ourselves and others, the sympathy we seek, the judgments we render about ourselves and others. They show up in our sometimes desperate efforts to prove our worth or gain self-esteem with possessions, titles, authority, control, accomplishments, etc. They show up in the patterns of our life, the repeating circumstances, the similar pains and results, the familiar relationships, the ongoing dysfunctions, over and over. They show up in what we settle for, our resignation to what we have, our hopelessness of having anything different. They show up in our dogged determination to be right about our weaknesses and victimhood and our inability to rise up, take charge of our life, and make something different out of it. And on and on.

And. . .*they are **WRONG**!*

Now I don't want to engage in a "right/wrong" game, but *you* are the one who decided to believe this stuff. While the small child may have perceived supporting evidence back then, perceived through the immature resources of the child, and concluded the beliefs that brought sense to a nonsensical world back then, it is now time to question whether they still apply to a grown up you in the present!

Is it possible that you have been living under a *Deception* all these years? Is it possible that you really are capable of doing incredible things; capable of creating marvelous results; capable of having relationships that work; capable of bringing satisfaction and growth to yourself and others?

Is it possible that you *can* live an Empowered Life in the face of all the habitual feelings and doubts and fears that have run your life since childhood? Is it possible that you can let go of the stuff you experienced back then, *even the abuse and perpetrations,* and walk on in your life cleansed from your past baggage? Is it possible that you *really are OK*, even that you are *magnificent and unconditionally accepted and loved* by the kind Universe that gave you existence? Is it possible that that Universe is simply waiting, patiently, for you to rise out of the mud hole of your perceived victimhood, the prison of your disempowered beliefs, and accept responsibility for your life? Is it possible that you can acknowledge the deception of smallness and inadequacy and *risk discovering your possibilities?* Is it possible that you can soar free as an **Eagle** and take on the awesome task of discovering and manifesting your incredible magnificence! Well, is it?

Welcome **Owl**! Welcome to the medicine of ultimate truth.

For me it took the pain of a relationship, a pain so bright that I could no longer deal with it outside of myself by blame and finger pointing at her. What will it take for you? **Owl** doesn't care. **Owl's** job is to get *your* attention to the deception *you* concluded as the foundation for your life. And all the other deceptions you created and believed as the details of your perceived Reality. **Owl** is patient, but **Owl** is persistent. If your attention is not gained by one challenge, you may be assured another opportunity will come along. Probably bigger and better. The **patterns** of your life contain the deceptions. And the patterns persist. Look into the patterns. **Owl** only wants you to pay attention, and notice the patterns.

Bear medicine is introspection, looks-within. Bear hibernates half the year in the cave. Then Bear wakes up, in the cave, and calls to us from the cave, **"Wake up!"** It is like we have been hibernating half our lives in the cave of our life. Once Owl has your attention, Bear initiates the invitation to engage in the transformation process. Bear invites you to Wake Up and *come into the cave of your life* where you can do the work.

Bear works together with **Owl**, in the West where the sun sets. **Owl** is a creature of the night. **Owl** wings fly silently. **Owl** hunts up close. **Owl** eyes see keenly in dark places. **Owl** comes into our life in the dark places, sometimes silently, surprising us. **Owl** always comes in the pains, challenges, and adversities. But maybe it takes the roar of **Bear** to get us going. Whether it takes the sharp pain of **Owl's** talons penetrating deep into our soul or the loud roar of **Bear** to look within, getting your attention is the only thing that matters. For the person seeking the Empowered Life, whatever gets the process going is a positive and valuable blessing. Be grateful.

Coming out of deception is scary. **Owl** is superstitiously feared by many of the native people as a bringer of death. Indeed something must die, but it is not the body. *It is the deception!* **Owl** is the messenger of Ultimate Truth. But the process is scary. If this pitiful creature that I have always believed to be the true me is really a deception; if I really am a magnificent, capable human being; if I really do deserve to respect and love myself; if I really can create wonderful results in my life, I have no experience of such a creature. If

I give up the old pitiful me, the victim, the manipulator, the seeker of sympathy, the controller, the power monger, and all the other strategies I have used to salvage a little esteem out of life, who is left?

Who am I when I stand naked in the center of the stage of my life, without all the familiar scripts and costumes and props and programmed responses and behaviors, interacting in programmed and directed ways with all the other actors in my little drama of life? Am I willing to make some mistakes, even public ones, while I work at learning who I am and owning myself as a capable, lovable, and worthy person? Am I willing to risk making a fool of myself while I explore being a magnificent human being? To experience embarrassment or endure mistakes? What if I screw up?

Ah, life! So many shrink from this opportunity because they fear that it will just add more stuff to that huge pile of condemnations they hide behind their Wall of Shame and Guilt, that it will just add more proof that they are Right about their weakness and smallness, about their not-OK-ness! What about you? Are you willing to take that risk? *You have to decide.* It is your life.

You either risk the possible discovery of magnificence, or you get to keep the same old life that you have always lived. You have two choices. Risk or sameness. Pick one!

You either create your life proactively or you create it <u>by default</u>. But *you create it* either way. Proactive choice or default choice. Pick one!

You either risk making mistakes in exploring the unexplored, by moving into uncharted territory, by developing and expressing the magnificent you, or you stay safe in the known, stuck with what you have always had. Pick one!

You either entertain the idea that you have been wrong about your entire victim-centered belief system and consider a new and unfamiliar possibility of capability and magnificence, or you cling stubbornly to being Right in the Reality you have. Pick one!

You either put this book down and give up the journey, or you hang in there with the stamina of **Elk**, keep reading, keep working, and face the magnificent potential in your life. Pick one!

It's your life. Decide!

Perhaps you might find it useful to list below some of the deceptions (limiting beliefs about yourself) that you see have held you back in your life. What risks have you been afraid to take? What fears have held you back? On the other hand, what risks can you take to break out of the prison of these limitations and beliefs? Be specific! Which of these risks are you *actually committed to take?* Get real! And be exhaustive in your listing!

-Notes to Self-

Chapter Five—

Unconditional

On the wooded land where we do the outdoor personal empowerment programs of the ropes course and firewalk, there live three owls that have been there for many years. One day at the beginning of a ropes course, my team and the leadership of the client group had circled up. I asked for some sharing on why each person was there and what each wanted to contribute to the experience of the soon-to-arrive participants. One woman immediately responded, "Unconditional love." At that exact moment one of the owls flew directly over our circle, in the daylight, not fifteen feet above the ground. **Owl** medicine, the medicine of deception!

Unconditional love. Unconditional acceptance. Unconditional friendship. Unconditional. What a word! How casually spoken! How often used! How little understood and lived.

Unconditional. Without conditions. Without *ANY* conditions. With *NO* conditions. None at all. Not one! *UNconditional!*

That is a tough concept to get our *conditional* minds around. We talk about giving each other unconditional love. We talk about receiving unconditional love from God. We talk about giving God unconditional love. *What a deception!* No wonder **Owl** flew over at that exact moment, to get our attention to it! We don't even have an internal framework to comprehend what Unconditional Love is!

My favorite passage in all of scripture is in the New Testament, Matt. 22: 36-40. It tells of an incident in which a lawyer asked Jesus a question. His purpose was to trip Jesus up, to catch him in a paradox. He asked which of all the commandments is the great commandment of the law.

Jesus' answer gives incredible insight into personal growth and empowerment. In answering, I believe Jesus used a profound teaching technique, simply and carefully designing his answer so that the lawyer would be confounded and even any of his disciples who were in the lawyer's frame of mind or context would be satisfied with their own rightness. How about you? What is your frame of mind?

He started off with the "obvious" (which would leave the lawyer "right" in his own paradigm, and Jesus' listeners in his entourage "right" in theirs) and then buried his real point way down at the end of the answer (where those who "had ears to hear" might find it). Jesus answered, "Thou shalt love the Lord thy God with all thy heart, and with all thy soul, and with all thy mind. This is the first and great commandment. And the second is like unto it, Thou shalt love thy neighbor as thyself. On these two commandments hang all the law and the prophets."

Let me take a little liberty with a few words in the King James Version and substitute "unconditionally" for "all thy heart," etc. The answer then teaches that the first commandment is to love God unconditionally, *And The Second* is to love your neighbor unconditionally, as you love yourself unconditionally. With his real point down there at the end (Thou shalt love *thyself unconditionally*), we see that keeping this commandment requires that we have an *internal frame of reference* for unconditional.

Until I can come to love and accept **myself** unconditionally, meaning _NO_ conditions, *right now,* including all my mistakes and weaknesses, including all the stuff I don't like about myself, in my mistakes and weaknesses, with my mistakes and weaknesses, knowing my mistakes and weaknesses, even knowing that God knows my mistakes and weaknesses, standing before the mirror in my own sight, naked with everything about me exposed, my behaviors, my thoughts, my feelings, my lusts, everything, **And *Accept Myself With It All,* And *Love Myself With It All, As I Am, Unconditionally,*** I have no internal frame of reference by which I can even see my neighbor as OK! Read this paragraph over and over until you really get it!

For everything I cannot accept in myself, *I will see in my neighbor.* The judgments I heap on myself, *I will heap on my neighbor.* The condemnations I lay on myself, *I will lay on my neighbor.* In fact, in my neighbor *I will perceive a mirror of the judgments and faults through which I really and subconsciously see myself.*

In unconditionality, there is no room for self-righteousness. So until I have come to that place where I can truly love and accept <u>myself</u> unconditionally, *Not One Condition*, as a human being, in *all* of my humanity, I am not prepared to extend that to my neighbor in his/her humanity. And until I have it worked out within myself, *and between me and my neighbor,* I have <u>no frame of reference</u> by which I can comprehend that God can love and accept me unconditionally! And I will continue to believe that God judges me and rejects me for my "mistakes," refusing to comprehend and acknowledge the *unconditional* love of God.

To accept myself unconditionally in the midst of my weaknesses and messes is not to condone either the weaknesses or the messes. However, it is to say, right now, ***<u>I'm OK! I'm Just Not Finished!</u>***

What a teaching! In one stroke, Jesus points the direction and focus of our entire life journey, and subtly hints that a patient Creator watches our struggles along that journey, not with judgment and condemnation, but with true unconditional love and encouragement. A patient Creator who wants us to love ourselves, unconditionally!

Welcome to the Human Race. Welcome home!

-Notes to Self-

Chapter Six—

The Inner-Directed Life

My father was not a religious man. I don't know that he would have even considered himself a spiritual man. He rarely sat me down to teach me about his personal philosophies. But I remember clearly one time when he did sit me down. I was probably nine or ten years old. He sat me down and said, "Cameron, people ought to live good, not because they want to go to Heaven, but because it's the way to live!" Wow!

Those words sank in and have stuck with me, in exactness, all these decades. It took many years for me to appreciate their powerful meaning. In those few words, my father taught me his philosophy of life. His life was the textbook example from which I could learn the meaning of what he shared with me. He walked his talk. He lived as honest a life as I have ever witnessed. He showed kindness and love to my mother beyond most of what I have seen and experienced elsewhere. His word was his bond. My father came from parents who lived by the same philosophy. I have had associates criticize these perceptions of my father as the idealistic perceptions of a child, but those words contain an important anchor to my heritage. It took decades for me to realize that my father and his parents lived an Inner-Directed Life.

Eventually I found that philosophy again in **Crow**. **Crow** medicine is the medicine of Law, not the law of government or society, but the law that governs us from within our Belief System; that inner law upon which we base our choices and decisions; the conscious *and* *subconscious* law that drives our behaviors and interactions with others; the law that determines our ethics, our values, and our relationship with our Universe.

If we look at the form of the law within us, the form it has when it rises into our consciousness and exercises control over our choices and behaviors, that form will tell us the source of the law within our lives. If it has the form of "supposed to," we know it comes from *outside* of us. I'm supposed to act this way. I'm supposed to believe this way. I'm supposed to think this way. I'm supposed to dress, work, marry, and live this way.

We follow the "supposed to" law *by obedience*. This is not to say it is wrong, only that our "supposed to" frame of reference for living comes from outside of us. It comes from government, society, culture, scripture, religion, etc. If we trace those outside sources back far enough we will come to the original source of "supposed to" in our life. It was our mother.

Our mother was the first human being with whom we had intimate contact in mortality. We were dependent on her. She represented safety and sustenance. And she was bigger than we were. She was our first and primary model for a Belief System or paradigm based on outside authority. The world in which we found ourselves was *her* reality. Her wish became *our* reality. From this primal relationship, the habitual frame of reference for our choices and behaviors in life was established as outside of us, in some authority figure, in something bigger than we, in "supposed to."

What form in our thoughts and words might the law have if it came from within us instead of from outside of us? It would have the form *"want to."* Now we begin to understand how we developed the habit of selling out "want to" in favor of "supposed to" in our life. For the early years of our life, when "want to" arose, it often came into conflict with "supposed to." Under our mother's imposition of her "supposed to," it became the habit of our life to ignore our "want to" or to devalue it. What I want is less important than what I am supposed to want. What I want to have is less important than what I am supposed to want to have. How I want to behave is less important than how I am supposed to want to behave. How I want my relationships to be is less important than how I am supposed to want my relationships to be. The conflict has been settled.

We have come to accept what we are supposed to want in our lives and have stopped looking for what we might actually want. We may have completely lost our ability to recognize what we actually want and can find only what we are supposed to want. We have *sold out our soul* to the beliefs and expectations we are *supposed to have*.

We have resigned ourselves to life as we are supposed to have, do, believe, and live it.

But my father suggested that "want to" might be positive. He taught me by his life that one can have a frame of reference that resides inside of self, a true inner law, one that provides real and meaningful internal boundaries for choices and decisions. It took me decades to realize what that was for him, and it is so simple!

My father's internal law was founded on Respect. It was a *highly boundaried life,* by choice. Think about that, *a highly boundaried life, by choice!* He accepted himself and he respected himself. From my father's life, I realized that if a "want to" came into his mind that would have been disrespectful *to him* or brought harm or shame *to him*, he did *not need to choose it.* He had an *internal boundary* with respect to himself. If a "want to" came into his mind in his relationship with another that would have been disrespectful to himself *or to the other*, he did not need to choose it. He had an *internal boundary* with respect to others. Even if that other person had no such internal frame of reference or boundary, my father had one that guided him in his life and he could deal with his world and everyone in it on the basis of his own inner law, a chosen law that had boundaries defined by respect. Especially, he had an internal boundary with respect to his wife, my mother. In his later years, he sent me a letter outlining the basis for their half-century relationship. It boiled down to *Respect.*

"People ought to live good, not because they want to go to Heaven, but because it's the way to live!" My father *chose* honesty, integrity, kindness, love, temperance, not because government or society or culture or religion told him he was supposed to, not because he believed God told him he was supposed to, but because *he wanted to!* It was what worked in the world he wanted to live in and *he created his experience of that world proactively* by the way he chose to live in it. And the woman he chose to spend his life with shared both this point of view and his values! There is the Mirror Principle applied to relationship!

Hey, is it really that easy? No, it is not always easy. Life has its joys and its pains. I don't have my father on an ivory tower. My father was a human being and had his human foibles. My father could not always avoid the pains or the perpetrators. But he *could always choose* how he dealt with them! And he did not always avoid making mistakes. But for the most part, he set an example of dealing with mistakes, pain, perpetrators, and fatherhood well, because he wanted to.

I suppose every world religion teaches in some form, maybe as a "supposed-to," the simple principle by which my father lived by choice. In the Western World, we have come to call it The Golden Rule. "Do unto others as you would have them do unto you." In the world of "supposed to," how many people can recite that principle word for word (in fact are "supposed to" be able to recite it!) and how many *actually live it?* How would it be to live in a world where Respect for Self and Respect for Others *actually guided* our behaviors and interactions because people chose to live that way? How would it be to live in a family where Respect for each other guided behaviors and interactions, where words spoken came from a deep sense of Respect and concern?

The *Real* Golden Rule *is an Inner Law*, and a truly Empowered Life is guided by that Inner Law. My father *wanted* to live a good life, not in hope of some reward in the afterlife, but because it was simply the way he wanted to live. It worked for him! It was the world in which he wanted to live and he did his part *to create that reality around him* by living it himself. I experienced that world in the family where I was raised.

But, you say, what if one is not raised in such a family and taught such "lofty" principles by such a father? What if, instead, father or mother or both were disrespectful or abusive, and one learned a belief system rooted in "supposed to," perhaps even harsh "supposed to" and inconsistency? What if one's very family contains perpetrators who inflect disrespect and abuse on one another? How does one then lift oneself out of the hell of the past to an Empowered Life in the present?

The answer is simple. *Get over it! Handle it!* (Oh gosh, Cam, there you go again making it simple!) I repeat, *Get over it! Handle it!*

That was then, *this is now*. Get out of the past. Grow up! Make a choice now to rebuild your life on a new habit. Is that a brutal answer? Maybe so, maybe not. You decide if it is brutal, or practical. It's your life! You can continue to live in the past, in anger and self-pity, with hatred and self-loathing, or you can get over it, get present, and move on toward Empowerment! Frankly, I don't believe the Universe cares about your past stuff or your attitudes about it. It's your life. *You* are the one who ought to care! What do *You* want to do about it?

To shift to an inner-directed life, <u>first</u> notice every time the old "supposed to" habit comes into your consciousness (and it comes every time you are tempted to make a choice or decide to act *based on "supposed to,"* including every time you find yourself feeling unworthy and undeserving; do you hear that voice from the past?), <u>and then</u> pause and make an adult decision on whether the "supposed to" choice is appropriate in present circumstances or represents your best adult judgment in dealing with them. Make an adult decision on whether you can recognize an appropriate "want to" option within yourself. Then choose your next move from *within yourself.*

"Supposed to" is not necessarily bad or inappropriate. Empowerment or disempowerment has to do with *inner motives and inner state,* not particular actions and results. BE-DO-HAVE! Pleasing others or pleasing God in hope of reward or recognition may be a lower motive than simply living a good life because it is the way to live. Even those lower motives may have positive results!

There are those who believe that morality and moral choices *require* religious or cultural influence and direction. I do not believe that to be true. My father showed me that moral choices have their own intrinsic motives and rewards. An inner directed life is just as valid, perhaps even more so, as an outer directed "supposed to" life. The results are the same but the motives are different. The Inner Directed Life comes from a true inner law and derives from inner directed choice, an internalized Golden Rule, inner Empowerment. Honesty, kindness, integrity are also found in "supposed to," and I respect moral choices based on such imposed teachings. And I respect even more the same choices based on the inner *want to* law!

My father lived the way he did because to him it was the way to live. It was, for him, an *internal law,* a "want to," and had nothing to do with anything outside of him. He lived it not because God wanted him to, but because HE wanted to. Empowerment and satisfaction are inner experiences of life. <u>They are attributes of a State of Being, not a</u>

state of doing or having. (Maybe you ought to pause and reflect on that last sentence! The **BE, DO, HAVE** of living!)

Much of the "supposed to" stuff that we blindly allow to direct our lives is *NOT* grounded in "the way to live." It is simply family, cultural and religious expectations, traditions, forms, habits, rituals. It may or may not add anything to the Empowered Life. One who chooses an Empowered Life is guided from within and *chooses* the law that guides oneself. An Empowered Life may learn from its own mistakes and messes to refine the internal law. That is good. And so we learn and grow. The idea has been expressed that when in Rome, do as the Romans do. I believe this idea teaches about Respect, not about "supposed to." I suspect that when one is not in Rome, there is no need to follow the particular forms and beliefs of the Romans. And even in Rome, one can courteously honor one's own inner law, even when invited otherwise by the Romans. So the Empowered Life is respectful, but will not sell out to inappropriate "supposed tos" just to be accepted or to please. The inner law is *a higher law* in that regard!

Thank you, father. It took me a long time to appreciate what you taught me as a boy. And I have found, as you did, that it is not always easy to live my life on the basis of internal principles. It takes courage and commitment and sometimes requires making tough choices in the face of disapproval or temptation, not because God is watching, but because *I* am watching! Not because I am accountable to God, but because I am accountable to *ME!*

Perhaps it might be useful to list below several "supposed to's" that you can identify in your life. Then notice how, and why, you are obedient with respect to them. Examine your motives for following them. Is it for the approval of others or the approval of God? Is it with the hope or expectation of a reward here or in the afterlife? This is not to say that that is wrong. This is a looks-within exercise with **Bear** for understanding your inner motivations. From such awareness comes choice. After you have identified several, find several more! You may be surprised how much your life is directed by external "supposed to's."

-Notes to Self-

Chapter Seven—

Ownership and Self-Esteem

Claiming an Empowered Life doesn't necessarily happen all at once. We build it step-by-step, realization-by-realization. It must be founded on the First Realization of Empowerment, accepting responsibility for it all. That is the first and most fundamental realization. But experiences of life continue to provide additional opportunities to learn. Someone once said to me, "How come I know I still have things to learn in my life? Because I am still on the planet!" That idea has become a mantra for me. *"I'm OK! I'm just not finished!"*

Moose, the Medicine of Self-Esteem, is the largest and loudest of the deer family. **Moose** stands on the top of the hill and bellows out, "I am Moose!" He bellows out a simple truth. Not in arrogance, but in simple ownership of who he is. Without shame or hiding, **Moose** declares the truth of his existence. In the spirit of **Moose**, one says without shame or false modesty, "This is who I am and this is what I do. I do it well because it comes from who I am." Then looking at the well-doing of another, says, "I don't do *that* well, but *that* is not me. It is someone else." In the spirit of **Moose**, we look at each other without envy or jealousy, but with respect and honor for who each of us is and how each of us expresses our being. We look at ourselves, at who we are as incredible human beings—bundles of potential, some developed and expressing, some yet to be developed and waiting to be expressed, but all magnificent and OK.

The male **Moose** bellows from the hilltop for the moose cow! **Moose** is not ashamed of any part of himself. He is not ashamed of nor does he hide his sexuality. It is a natural expression of himself, as appropriate in its season as all other expressions in their seasons. It falls to the humans, in our so-called "higher consciousness," to find shame in aspects of ourselves. This is probably a unique and disempowering quality of humans among all the creatures of the Universe.

Back in the 70s I remember the outcry from some of the self-righteous when the Voyager missions were searching for a design for the plaque to be mounted on the vehicles (which, by the way, are now outside the planets of our solar system and on their way into interstellar space!). The plaque on the vehicle was proposed to provide an image of its makers, human beings, male and female, the species that made this craft, for any other inhabitants of the Universe who might happen to encounter it in its eternal journey through space. The proposed image showed a simple line sketch of two naked human figures, male and female. The outcry focused on how sinful and disgusting it is to show an uncovered human body!

Ah, the world of "supposed to." **Moose** stands on the hilltop, unashamed of any aspect of his being, proclaiming himself to all creatures of the Universe, and inviting the moose cow to share in the joy of being. Can you feel a bit of pride in the possibility that some other intelligent beings might someday find that vehicle and see who we are, proclaiming ourselves to be its creators? We did this! See us!

Can you begin to feel the pride of accepting who you are as a marvelous human being? Not a negative or puffed up pride, but a positive pride coming from a new view of yourself as a beautiful, worthy, capable member of the incredible human race, right now, just as you are; a pride that cleanses and motivates you to shine forth in your magnificence; a pride that encourages you unashamedly to take risks to explore your magnificence; a pride that empowers you to search for new growth opportunities and avenues to express your unique gift to the world.

I strongly believe that each human being is totally unique. There are no two of us who are exactly alike. Ever before, ever now, or ever again. You and I are each one-of-a-kind in all of space and time! Even genetically identical twins live individual lives and possess unique gifts to discover and give to the world. Even in twin-hood, separate spirits occupy genetically identical physical bodies, each rendering its life unique among all lives ever lived. Every one of us has a unique expression of self that, discovered and given, makes a difference in the world. Maybe the world we influence is a small circle or a large circle, maybe contained within a family or a village, or extends to wider portions of humanity, but our world is made a bit different because we found that gift and gave it. No life is devoid of meaning. Our opportunity in life is to find that meaning and express it.

People have actually said to me, "I don't have any *real* talents." They are usually referring to performing or artistic talents like music or painting or such. What a shame to define talents so narrowly. What a shame to limit the search for self because of a limiting belief about the smallness of self.

A talent could also be defined as that unique expression of self that, developed and given, makes a difference in the world. And the world affected could be defined as simply the life of one other person. To have lived and given that unique gift to one other person is to have made a difference in the world because you were here. Think of Helen Keller, and that one other person, Annie Sullivan, who reached through Helen's "disability" and unleashed her potential. How many countless people have been influenced by Annie Sullivan's gift to that one person? I'll bet you have been influenced in some way by Helen Keller!

Think of the devoted mother or father, whose devotion to one child allowed that child to grow up to bless others, and how far those ongoing blessings reach. Think of your ancestors who perhaps courageously dealt with challenge and difficulty in their little part of the world, and raised their children through it to create posterity. One of whom continued on, whose posterity eventually gave life and opportunity *to you!* How many individual gifts were expressed, person by person, generation by generation, in that long and great lineage that resulted in you? And how many individuals are alive today and making their difference in the world because one of those gifts was given along the way? This is worth pondering! And expressing some gratitude!

The Empowered Life is not defined in terms of fame or noted accomplishment. It is defined in terms of inner choices and attitudes. If one Empowered Life served only as an example to another and that other life chose empowerment, and that other raised a family of children who chose empowerment, and families and communities and nations were eventually affected, how did that one person's quiet gift, perhaps unknown or unrecognized even to the one who gave it or to the one who received it, eventually change the world? If one mother teaches her child to value herself and own her life, and that child grows up to embrace an Empowered Life—passing that precious gift down from generation to generation, how much has that one mother made a difference in the world? The decision you make today to pursue empowerment may have profound and far-reaching consequences beyond your wildest imaginings, even way beyond your own lifetime. It is a decision very much worth making!

There resides in the North, beside Wisdom and **Moose**, another creature with powerful medicine. It is **Buffalo**. Nations of native people made their entire way of life around the buffalo. The herds of buffalo could not be numbered. Yet they provided the very sustenance of the people. Food, clothing, shelter, tools, toys, healing, virtually every necessity of life was made available to the people from these mighty herds. And in appreciation for their importance to the people, when the plains peoples hunted the buffalo, they first gave thanks to these creatures before taking their lives.

Buffalo is a very sacred medicine to the plains peoples. Where many of the medicine creatures in the circle carry only one medicine, **Buffalo** carries two. **Buffalo** medicine teaches us of Prayer *and* Abundance. Prayer given for all the Abundance life provides.

From **Buffalo** we learn something amazing. **Buffalo** teaches us the Prayer of Gratitude. To the seeker of the Empowered Life, in this simple teaching lies an incredible Principle.

In the world religions, I suppose that one of the highest virtues taught is the virtue of unconditional forgiveness (that word "unconditional" again). By forgiving ourselves and by forgiving those who have trespassed against us, we relieve ourselves and the perpetrators of the burden of the trespass. We notice here that the virtue of forgiveness *implies a trespass*. It implies *a wrong* done against us, a perpetration.

Buffalo teaches that there is yet a *higher principle*. It is the Principle of Gratitude. Gratitude is an incredible principle that comes *in the North*, near the end of the healing process. To those still in the South of the journey, engaging with **Porcupine** and Vulnerability, it may seem ridiculous. To those who are still dealing with **Owl** in the West, it may appear as folly and unreachable. Only after we have engaged with **Bear** and **Owl** *and* accepted complete responsibility for our life does the Principle of Gratitude begin to emerge as the ultimate Healing Principle. It comes after we have taken on the life issues illuminated in this round of our journey of healing and empowerment. It comes after we have learned the lessons offered by **Porcupine** and **Owl**, laid aside some core deceptions, and come to the self-acceptance and self-esteem of **Moose**. It is a gift *added to* those lessons in our expanding sense of self. *The Principle of Gratitude renders forgiveness unnecessary and irrelevant.*

Here is how the Principle of Gratitude works. As we look back over the journey, we note the struggles and challenges of **Owl**. We note how they came to us through the pains and adversities of life, the people and circumstances that we had to deal with, the perpetrators who abused us and treated us disrespectfully, the anger and resentment we felt and with which we had to come to grips, the baggage of the past that we let go, important life lessons we learned from these experiences. We note how we grew in strength and knowledge of our ability to deal with life and to prosper through these challenges. We note how we would have *missed the lessons* had these people and circumstances not been in our life *exactly as they were!* We then realize that what we once held as a trespass against us was *really a blessing!* The Universe, in its kind and loving way, gave us a perfect set of circumstances so we could learn the lessons we most needed to learn and gain the strength we most needed to gain. We are then filled with gratitude for the valuable and perfect path of growth we were given, including *every circumstance* along the way.

Thank you, Universe, for sending **Owl** to get my attention. *Thank you, Universe,* for the struggles and challenges of my life and my opportunities to learn and grow. And *thank you, Universe,* for the lessons learned. When the Principle of Gratitude comes, forgiveness becomes irrelevant and unnecessary because we no longer perceive ourselves as wronged. Rather we see how we were blessed, and in that new perception, we take ourselves to a higher plane. But it is a North Principle and considered too soon, is perceived as folly. The Journey is laid out in the map. Follow it from East all the way around the circle to the North. Work the process step by step through the South and the West. Engage with **Porcupine** and **Owl**, find **Moose**. Then let the

Principle of Gratitude flow through you naturally as you step gratefully and joyfully into the Empowered Life.

As **Eagle** flies with us throughout the journey to keep us in touch with the Spiritual Nature of the healing process and give us courage to continue the journey, so there is that other creature of the North who watches over us. It is **Elk**. **Elk** medicine is stamina. As **Elk** survives its predators by pacing itself and continuing on, so **Elk** watches over us from the North. When we look into the cave of the East and see our life issues illuminated by current circumstances and pains and want to run away and avoid, **Elk** says, hang in there, take it on. As we encounter **Porcupine** and our Wall of Shame and Guilt, and want to run away and hide in our shame, **Elk** says, hang in there, keep going. As we accept the invitation of **Bear** to go into the cave of the West and deal with the issues of life, and we feel the talons of **Owl** in our souls and have to face our deceptions and want to run away and give it up, **Elk** says, hang in there; keep going. The North is just ahead.

And finally, there is **Coyote**, the trickster, who has no home on the circle but roams with us, laughing. **Coyote** says to us, as we get caught up in the seriousness of life and its pains and struggles, and feel so victimized by the unfairness of life and want to blame circumstances and others, "Don't take yourself and life so seriously." Smile at life. Find the positive in every lesson. Look forward to the Empowered Life, beyond the issues, with hope and encouragement. Laugh at yourself. After all, you created it! That pitiful, victimy creature who actually believed that it took manipulation and control and approval and attention and drama and all that other stuff of addiction and deception to have meaning in life, *is you!* After all, it is pretty funny, isn't it?

In the movie, The Wizard of Oz, Dorothy stood watching the humbug wizard fly off in the balloon, feeling hopeless of ever having her wish granted to return home to Kansas. The Good Witch of the North, arriving in her bubble, pointed out that Dorothy had had her desires all along. She was wearing the ruby slippers, and had been wearing them throughout her journeys in *Oz*! All she had to do was tap the ruby slippers together three times and recite, "There's no place like home. There's no place like home. There's no place like home."

It was amazing to Dorothy that it was so simple. She had had her desires all along! And *you* have had yours all along, too. All *you* have to do is make a decision; choose a new Reality, a new set of beliefs and expectations of yourself, one based on owning your life and your magnificence, and being willing to risk the discovery of who you are as a magnificent human being. Tap *your* shoes together three times and recite, "I'm OK! I'm OK! I'm OK!" Welcome to the journey. Welcome home!

And if you don't believe it is that simple, **Coyote** will keep laughing, ***and keep biting you in the butt!***

Perhaps you might find it useful to list below some of your unique strengths and attributes. Also list some of the blessings of Owl (the challenges, pains, and struggles of the past) for which you are now grateful because of how they contributed to your growth! There is lots of space, for there are lots to list!

-Notes to Self-

Section Three—
Applying the Simple Principles of Empowerment

Chapter Eight—

Results or Stories

We get exactly two things out of life: Results or Stories. We either get what we set out to create, or we get stories and excuses about why we failed. That's it. One or the other. Which do you usually pick?

Come on now. Don't try to get around it. You have either results in your life or you have your stories and excuses. The problem is, most of us end up *believing* our stories! The reason I didn't accomplish such and such, or get such and such, or experience such and such, is the weather, or the people I was working with, or the market. My boss is a crumb, or my spouse is to blame, or my kids are unruly, etc., etc., etc. Life isn't fair!

Whine, cry, blame, excuse, tell stories for sympathy, gossip for a shred of esteem, hide in alcohol and drugs, manipulate, control, seek approval, run your dramas for attention, substitute sex and all manner of other addictive dramas and behaviors for love, and all the other strategies you employ to try to salvage some shreds of self-esteem, "feels good," and meaning out of your pitiful life. And failing that, you resort to bigger and better dramas and strategies. Surely more and bigger and louder and more dramatic will give you what you so desperately seek. Surely the "feels good" substitutes you cling to, the "fixes" for your addictions, will satisfy your cravings for real self-love and real self-esteem. Surely. . . .(Ah, enters **Coyote!**)

"If you keep on doing what you've always done, you keep on getting what you've always got."

"The definition of insanity is continuing to do the same thing, expecting a different result."

These are the mantras for the treatment of addiction!

So take a look. A real look. A brutally honest look. A brutally honest look in the mirror of your life. What are the results in your life? I don't mean the car, the house, the job, or the pay. While that stuff is part of the picture, look at the deep stuff. Look at your own view of yourself, your self-definition. Look down inside your heart. Look at how you feel about your accomplishments, your experience of your relationships. Look at what drives you in your choices and actions. Look at your self-talk, the chatter of your mind. Look at your habits, your addictions, *including your addictions to image, control, approval, acceptance, attention, sympathy, gossip, sex*. Look at how willing you are to sell-out your soul for those little "fixes," those little "feels goods." Look at your self-judgments, the stuff you are ashamed of, the stuff you wouldn't want your spouse or your kids or your friends and associates to know was there in your mind, or on your computer hard drive, or in your website searches. Look into the little secret, private places about which only you know. Look at your feelings, your fears, your anxieties, your sadness, and your despair. Your results are everywhere around you *and within you*. See them in life's mirror.

Now look deeper still. Look at the reasons you give yourself for what you have in your life. Look at your excuses and stories, your justifications. Notice the form they have. Notice things like blame, passions, the actions and behaviors of others, tough luck stuff, illness, disabilities. It's his fault, it's her fault, it's because of the weather, it's because of circumstances, it's because I am weak, incapable, unworthy, unlovable. It's because I am sick, disabled. It's because life isn't fair. Poor me. If only. . . .

Notice how often others, your boss or coworkers or spouse or neighbors or friends or even strangers figure in. Notice how the unexpected happenings in your life figure in, accidents, misfortunes, illness. If only. . . .

The Empowered Life notes the stories and recognizes them for what they are, just stories, excuses, reasons, and distractions from the real business of living and creating results. The Empowered Life then focuses on *the Two Most Important Questions in life:*

What do I want?

What price am I willing to pay to have it?

Most of us never *really* address the first question. We kid ourselves into believing that we address it. We set goals, make New Year resolutions, etc. We settle for "pipe dreams" instead of setting real goals. I'll bet your smart phone "to do lists" and your bottom drawer are full of old goals and "what-I-wants." It is a growing pile!

Would you like to know the answer to the first question, What do I want? OK, brace yourself.

What you want is what you have!

Perhaps more accurately stated, what you have is what you wanted to pay the price to have. It is what you *have wanted most* every time you made a choice to pay some price. That's it. You got it. You bought it. You have exactly what you paid the price to have in your life. You see, the second question is always answered in the first (Did **Owl** get your attention with that one?). You may not want to admit that you have exactly what you want. But the results indicate exactly the price you were willing to pay. If you want something different in your life, you have to be willing to pay a different price. It's that simple. What you have is an exact mirror of your priorities. Period.

Does life sometimes happen outside of this simple statement? Sure, you can wait for the lottery. And maybe you will win. But probably you will just live on. . . .waiting. For the vast majority of us, we have exactly what we bought with the price we were willing to pay—in your career, in your relationships, in your personal life, in your spiritual life. You have it. You have exactly what you bought. Get real. Take a look.

The *second question* has only *one answer* if the answer to the first question is *real*. What price am I willing to pay to have what I really want? ***Whatever it takes!*** *If this is what I **Really** want, then I will do whatever it takes to have it!*

Now reality sets in. I start to notice that when the actual price begins to present itself, mind chatter like, "I will do whatever it takes, *except*. . . ." Or, "I'll do whatever it takes, *if only* . . ." Or, "I'll do whatever it takes, *unless*. . . ." When the price becomes known, we get to get real with ourselves. "I guess I didn't really want it that bad."

Every condition you place on Whatever-
It-Takes *is more important to you* than what
you said you wanted. We can just shorten
Whatever-It-Takes to a little acronym, WIT.
That's the only price that matters if you are
clear and real about what you want! WIT. Do
you hear **Coyote** laughing again?

Which brings us to balance in life. This is another principle shown
to us in the Medicine Wheel.

Take the first question: What do I want? There are many facets to
life. Physical, professional, personal, family, spiritual, and many
others. How you rank these depends on your individual priorities, but
they are all part of the Empowered Life.

The Empowered Life addresses the question "What do I want?" in
the totality of one's life. To the Empowered Life, achieving balance is
critical because what I want is empowerment in the whole of my life
and includes all aspects, physical, professional, family, personal,
spiritual, etc. To commit a high portion of life's energy to achieving
what I want primarily in one area of life may leave other important
areas of life unaddressed. There are many broken marriages, broken
families, broken relationships, broken careers, unfulfilled dreams,
because one or both partners committed too much energy to narrow
areas of the total life picture. The balance of the Circle!

The Empowered Life recognizes that the choices of an inner-
directed life are not always easy and must be addressed in the largest
conceivable picture at a given moment of choice. The Empowered Life
avoids some traps and pitfalls I call set-ups for negative experiences.

Set-Ups for Negative Experiences in Life

Becoming too attached to specific outcomes

> When we define what we want in terms of specific physical or
> interpersonal outcomes, especially specific interpersonal
> outcomes, we set ourselves up for eventual disappointment. For
> example, let's say you believe what you want is that a particular

person fall in love with you and marry you. In such a case, *he/she* that you fawn upon has a specific name <u>and</u> *he/she* is a free agent and will make his/her own choice based on *his/her* own criteria. No matter how much you want it, nor what you do to bring it about, *he/she* may or may not make a corresponding choice. Perhaps better to define what you want in terms of the *attributes* of a desired partner and achieving a relationship that *has certain qualities* when you meet *him/her*. The answer to the question then guides you in your search for such a one.

But what about specific physical outcomes? For example, you invest all your energy in having that specific house at such and such an address. And then maybe another buyer comes along with a better or quicker offer or you don't happen to qualify for the financing. Or you want a specific job at a particular company. Perhaps better to define what you want in terms of the attributes of the house or job and the qualities of the neighborhood or company, keeping your eyes open for an available one that best matches your list.

The point is that you can answer the first question clearly in terms of the qualities and attributes you want and set yourself up for a positive outcome when you don't become too attached to a *particular* outcome. The broader you identify what you want, the greater the field of options that will satisfy it.

Defining what you want in terms of negative feelings about the past

"This is what I *don't want*." You are still in reaction to the past. You have not accepted it, not learned the lessons, and are not yet ready to move on to a truly Empowered Life. OK, so learn the lessons, note the patterns in the past, and move on to what you *do want* in the present and future.

There are countless examples of people, particularly women, who have a pattern of being in abusive relationships. Each time they leave one, they focus on *not being* in another one; they focus on the characteristics they *don't want* to find in a man. But rather than looking at the reasons for their own pattern and why they keep associating with a certain class or character of men, they just keep on doing just that. And, sure enough, they keep on getting what they focus on.

Focusing on what you don't want was one of the patterns that kept getting it for you back then! Strange, but true. Focus continually and carefully on not getting gravy on your tie or blouse and, sure enough, you will get gravy on your tie or blouse. You create what you focus on. I think it's one of Murphy's Laws!

Being Right about or being attached to some belief associated with what you say you want

This is a form of being attached to a specific outcome and narrows the field of possibilities, distracting you from getting what you really want when a perfectly good possibility comes along. For example, you believe you will only be happy if a *blonde* person falls in love with you. Or one with a certain figure or physique. Or you believe you will only be happy with a job with a certain starting salary or title. (These *are* just beliefs and are part of *your* definition of *your* specific reality.) Is this the reality you *really* want? Or is there a *much bigger* reality that you **Really** seek? Do your limiting beliefs keep you from seeing bigger possibilities. Suppose several possibilities come along for a loving and compatible partner who don't happen to match up with that limiting belief of hair color or figure. Suppose some very promising job opportunities show up that are hidden by that limiting commitment to starting salary or title. Our attachment to beliefs can us put in a prison that actually keeps us from having what we really want because we don't recognize it right there beyond the obscuring haze of our short sighted perceptions. Be willing to set aside beliefs from the past. It's a whole new life you are starting to build, a new reality defined by more positive, more expansive beliefs. Open yourself up to a universe of possibilities!

Let's suppose that you are quite clear on what you want and it fits together into a balanced picture (as best you can conceive at the present time; remember life is risk and the Empowered Life is continually learning and revising). Now go on to the second question: What price am I willing to pay to get it? WIT! (Are you smiling yet with **Coyote**?)

Whatever it takes! Just feel the energy of commitment surging inside you when you really comprehend *and own* what that means. You are willing to do *whatever it takes* to achieve what you want. You will pay any price. You commit every ounce of your entire being into the realization of your goal. The full majesty and magnificence of your entire Human Being is marshaled and focused. As a deserving, capable, magnificent Child of the Universe, you are absolutely dedicated to the achievement of this worthy objective, conceived from the depths of your desire and expressing your uniqueness and your gift to the world. *Whatever it takes,* to make your difference in the world, to leave your mark, to unleash the power that resides within you and your dreams. You feel your family shining and thriving because of your commitment and dedication. You see your personal or professional accomplishment shining and thriving because of your commitment and enthusiasm. Your connection with your Universe vibrates with energy. Your sense of yourself shines with confidence and commitment. You haven't even started yet, but you already glow in the accomplishment because you know who you are and that you are absolutely capable of, and committed to, bringing your dream into reality.

There is a little poster that hangs on many refrigerators and kitchen walls (at least that is where it hung in my home for several years). It is entitled "Commitment" and has been attributed to Goethe. It embodies the spirit of WIT!

Commitment

Until one is committed, there is hesitancy, the chance to draw back, and always ineffectiveness.

Concerning all acts of initiative (and creation), there is one elementary truth, the ignorance of which kills countless ideas and splendid plans: that the moment one definitely commits oneself, then Providence moves, too.

All sorts of things occur to help one that would never otherwise have occurred. A whole stream of events issues from the decision raising in one's favor all manner of unforeseen incidents and meetings and material assistance which no man could have dreamt would have come his way.

Whatever you can do, or dream you can, begin it.

Boldness has genius, power, and magic in it!

—*Taken from W. H. Murray in The Scottish Himalaya Expedition, 1951.*

Perhaps you might find it useful to list below some of your favorite stories and excuses. Be bold and honest with yourself. Note especially the stories you have come to actually *believe!* Then write down some of the things you say you want. If you don't have them yet, ask yourself what price you have not yet been willing to pay? There is not an infinite amount of energy available in most of our lives. Even the Empowered Life must narrow the range of wants to those worthy of the expenditure of Whatever It Takes! This is an opportunity to get real with yourself. The Empowered Life seeks truth and honesty. There is plenty of space to Get Real here!

-Notes to Self-

Chapter Nine—

The Prison of "You Make Me. . . ."

One of the most disempowering, victimy statements I know is "You make me mad!" You can substitute any of several other words for "mad," such as angry, sad, and offended, and it remains *victim*. To actually believe and declare that someone else "makes you" have any particular inner state is to believe and acknowledge to the world that someone else has power over you, that someone else's words or behaviors are more powerful than your ability to choose. In such a declaration and belief, you have literally given that person or group control over you! That is one of the *Great Deceptions* of life. **Owl** is sinking his talons into your soul. *No one makes you do anything. You choose to do it!*

Come on. Are you on a journey to empowerment or not?

Look back over the past few days. Have you allowed such disempowering thoughts or words to pass through your mind, or possibly even out of your mouth? Have you allowed someone else, through words or behaviors, to trigger you so that you lost all control over yourself and fell totally under the power of another? *You made me mad! You offended me!* And if not the last few days, how long has it been since you demonstrated such a lack of self-control? Blaming is one of the insidious habits *of victims!*

If you really want to experience empowerment, you must examine yourself and realize that *No One Else* can determine your internal state. Others can *only behave. Others Can Only Behave!* **OTHERS CAN ONLY BEHAVE!!** *You* always choose how you respond to their behaviors. *You Always Choose How You Respond To Their Behaviors!* This flies in the face of most of today's "politically correct" society! People do not do things to you; *they just do things!*

You offend me. You make me mad. What a position of victimhood! Another person's behavior controls your internal state and like a puppet on a string, you jiggle around and dance. You see, a dance is a set of coordinated and predictable actions. Partner A moves a certain way and Partner B moves in a specific corresponding way. The "dance of anger" or the "dance of offense" is exactly a dance between partners like any other dance. In the dance of life, Partner A behaves in a "triggering way" and Partner B reacts to the trigger in a corresponding, programmed, and reactive way by, say, getting mad. Of course, that invites Partner A to react in a correspondingly bigger way, and so the dance continues, getting more and more intense and pretty soon "off to the races!"

I believe that people who choose to live in community, like family and neighborhood, and that includes pretty much all of us, owe it to our community to learn and practice behaviors of kindness and respect for each other. That's what makes community work. That is the meaning of the "Golden Rule," treat others as you yourself would want to be treated. This simple principle applies to local communities as well as communities of city, state, nation, and even as human beings in the community of the world. We owe it to ourselves and our communities to practice it *and* teach it to our children. I have a responsibility to practice respectful behaviors toward you and you have the same responsibility to practice them toward me. This is to me a self-evident truth of living for anyone who chooses to live in the community of humankind!

However, if someone else does not behave kindly or respectfully towards me, that does not reduce or eliminate my responsibility, nor give me license to shirk mine! I do not *have to* engage in the dance. As an empowered person, *I have choice!* In fact the obvious choice is simply *Not To Dance.* The key here is to realize that I always have *Options* (remember Viktor Frankl?). What happens in a dance when one partner decides not to dance? The dance cannot continue. It has to stop!

So what are some options that I and all of us have to stop the dance? Getting mad is one option, perhaps the predictable one. Getting offended is one option, perhaps another predictable one. Other options include responding with kind words. Whoa! One person speaks an insult and the other responds with kindness? Might that disarm the other person who is used to believing that one insult results in another insult, or taking offense? The dance has to stop! How about just smiling and saying "Thank you." Another option! How about simply changing the subject? How about looking the other way or turning around? How about first smiling, and then leaving the room? How about. . . ? *There are an infinite number of options!* Remember Ghandi! Remember the Freedom Riders!

The key to having options in situations which may arise suddenly is to prepare your options in advance. Think about your associates, in your family, in your neighborhood, among your friends, at work. You can probably bring to mind specific people with whom you have had "dances" in the past. People who often demonstrate "triggering behaviors." Now think about yourself and things that have been "triggering behaviors" for you and have produced in you reactions of anger or offense. The patterns of your life. These people and these behaviors are likely to happen again, and you are likely to again be triggered into reaction, unless you prepare yourself *in advance* with several options so that when things show up that might trigger you into a dance, you draw from your list and simply exercise another option. Rehearse these options in your mind over and over so that you have a ready supply of them when a situation arrives suddenly. You don't then have to think them out. You simply respond with one or more that seem to be most suitable and most likely to ultimately achieve what you want in the relationship.

Remember, the key to empowerment is knowing what you want. Perhaps what you want most is an ongoing good relationship with the person who performs a "triggering behavior." Select an option that has the greatest likelihood of allowing the relationship to continue in a positive manner after the situation has passed. Getting mad or being offended are probably not options that are likely to promote your desired outcome.

That someone else speaks or behaves unkindly or disrespectfully toward you is **Not Your Problem**, *unless you choose to make it your problem*. It remains the problem of the other. An old saying is, "Your opinion of me is none of my business." An empowering decision you can make in life is one that results in you not taking on other people's problems regarding you. Hard? Only if you would rather have others control you and determine your feelings and internal state. Then it is hard. It's easy if you prepare for it, and practice it over and over in your life.

What would happen in our communities of family, neighborhood, nation, even world, if we as human beings could accept responsibility for our own internal state and learn this simple and empowering way to live together? Words like blame, revenge, payback, get even, would become irrelevant, and peace on earth might actually be achieved!

Perhaps you might find it useful to pause here and think about how you have been triggered into states of anger, offense, and other negative states. List below behaviors and words that have been triggers for you. Then think about and write down several options for each of the triggering people and situations that are available to you that have the potential of stopping the dance. Finally, rehearse these options in your mind several times so that you have them at ready to use in the future if you should again encounter such triggers.

 **-Notes to Self-**

Chapter Ten—

The Prison of "I Can't"

One of the great stories we tell ourselves is "I Can't." I can't do this because. . . ." And then we give ourselves an excuse or story. "I don't have the time." "I don't have the money." "I don't have the ability. . . ." The trouble is, we end up believing that our stories are true! Those listening to our stories may actually buy the story and thus *enable* us to stay stuck in our prison of disempowered victimhood with their sympathy. Come on now, let's think about this one. "I can't" is an affirmation of the *belief of incapability*. "I can't" is a prison of our own construction that keeps us contained within walls of self-denial. I am *incapable* as a human being of accomplishing this thing. I don't have *the ability* as a human being to accomplish this thing. *I'm not capable! I'm not enough!*

Come on now! You have the same human being as any other human being. The honest and truthful way to state our lack of desire to accomplish something is, "I don't want to," "I'd rather not," or "I won't." Take a look. You have all the faculties of a human being. You have a human brain, skills, physical, spiritual, and emotional resources. You have opportunities. You have the same amount of time as every other human being—24 hours a day, seven days a week, 365 days a year. Look at any person whom you perceive has accomplished amazing things. You have exactly the same amount of time available to you as that person does. The thing that prevents you from accomplishing results in your life is *your priorities*, not your capability or your resources!

"I am unwilling to invest more than so much time and energy in creating this result." That is an honest statement and places the thing in the realm of an empowered choice and you in the place of an empowered individual who makes such choices. In the spirit of "What Do I Want?" and an honest assessment of your willingness to pay the price to get it, you may be truly unwilling to pay a sufficient price. But to throw a smoke screen of "I can't" is to affirm that you are incapable as a human being. *You are holding yourself, your Creator, and the universe you live in as small.*

What a disempowering belief! You are *absolutely capable* as a human being and you have all the resources of *your human being*! There are countless examples of human beings with far less physical capabilities, mental and financial resources than you or I, who accomplish incredible results and have very satisfying lives. The difference is they don't live in the prison of "I can't." They tell themselves the truth about their priorities, live from that truth, and invest their energy accordingly. Think of Steven Hawking. Think of Viktor Frankl. Think of Helen Keller.

I knew a couple who were invited to a function weeks in advance. They responded, "We can't get a baby sitter." Come on folks. They are telling themselves a story that imprisons and disempowers them. They may not have wanted to go to the function. Just say so. Tell the truth. But to declare that they are *incapable* of finding a baby sitter with weeks advance notice is a joke! **Coyote** is laughing his head off!

I believe we who are striving to live Principles of Empowerment have some responsibility to support others in at least knowing they have some choices in their lives for empowerment. If we buy statements of "I can't" without any challenge, we *enable* the speaker to remain stuck in victimhood and smallness. Better to expect the truth than such a lie. Ask for the truth!

Why don't we rise to this level in our relationships? Is it because we don't want "to offend" or "to hurt feelings?" Go back to Chapter Nine. Go back to the Issues of Support in Applying the Principles of Growth. We are talking about the Enabling Issue here. Another one is the Approval/Acceptance Issue. Do we care enough about others to support them in rising out of victimhood to greater self-honesty and self-esteem? The world we live in is comprised of the people and circumstances that surround us. If we want to live in an empowered world, we have some responsibility to support ourselves *and others* to create that world!

Perhaps it might be useful for you to list below several circumstances in recent weeks where you have thought, maybe even expressed, "I can't." Get real with yourself in terms of the underlying issues here. What are your priorities such that you used this excuse as a smokescreen *to yourself?* Do you actually believe it? How has your continual use of this phrase sapped your self-esteem and power to accomplish? Is this a disempowering habit you have? How do you suppose the people who heard you say this feel about your attitude about your capability as a human being? Would it serve the relationship and future opportunities in it for you to go back and tell them the truth? Also consider your associates. How do you enable them to remain stuck in victimhood? How can you apply the Principles of Support in your relationships?

-Notes to Self-

Chapter Eleven—

The Prison of "I'm Afraid"

In the empowerment programs I run, there are activities that present participants with what might be perceived as quite intimidating challenges. For example climbing trees and jumping into mid-air for rings or walking barefoot across burning coals. These are very effective opportunities for personal growth and empowerment because they bring participants face to face with self-imposed barriers in their lives and allow them to make choices to deal with them.

We all live in a prison. The walls of that prison are based on the beliefs we hold about our capabilities in the Reality we constructed as infants and small children.

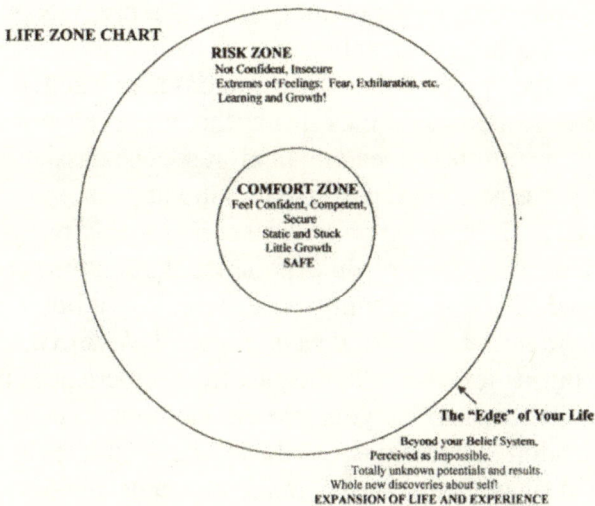

LIFE ZONE CHART

RISK ZONE
Not Confident, Insecure
Extremes of Feelings: Fear, Exhilaration, etc.
Learning and Growth!

COMFORT ZONE
Feel Confident, Competent,
Secure
Static and Stuck
Little Growth
SAFE

The "Edge" of Your Life
Beyond your Belief System.
Perceived as Impossible.
Totally unknown potentials and results.
Whole new discoveries about self!
EXPANSION OF LIFE AND EXPERIENCE

Most of us live our lives clinging to "Comfort Zone." We do everything we can to avoid risk, fear, feelings of discomfort, in fact any strong feelings. Think of the amount of energy you expend avoiding strong feelings, such as fear or embarrassment, thus staying comfortable in a place in your life that is known and predictable. There is *no growth there*, only staying stuck in the same-old results you have always experienced. I am not saying this is wrong, only that it does not lead to empowerment or great accomplishment. From the place of Comfort Zone, your life is very predictable and safe, probably very small compared to your potential.

The feeling we seem most to want to avoid is fear. Like "I Can't" in the last chapter, fear is a limiting component in the wall of our comfort zone prison that confines our life to smallness. Let's look at fear. It is a critical part of our arsenal of survival. If we did not feel fear, most of us would not have survived childhood. Now we are grown-ups. How does fear operate in our lives?

Fear is a feeling, a sensation, based on chemicals injected into our bloodstream from glands that are stimulated by inputs from our senses. That chemical is adrenaline. It is interesting to note that the *same chemical*, adrenaline, also produces excitement. What is the difference? It is the meaning we give to the input as it is filtered through our belief system (based on previous experience). This is a pretty good system for survival. Once *we* assign meaning to that feeling associated with that stimulus, we either prepare for flight, defense, or excited enjoyment! Each of these responses comes from the same chemical, with an experientially determined meaning and response, assigned with the resources we possessed in infancy and childhood.

Where is fear? It is *inside of us.* You can probably put your hand on the place *in your body* where *you* experience the sensation of fear. Fear is only a signal. There is nothing "out there," *only our perception of what is out there and the habitual meaning our beliefs assign to it.* Since you created your belief system in the past from experiences in your past, it is perfectly OK to examine your present circumstances in the light of present-time, adult perceptions, evaluate them in the light of adult capability to deal with them, and make an adult decision on how to proceed. There is a great book title, *Feel the Fear and Do It Anyway!* That title alone invites you to use your feeling of fear as a guide *and then* to examine the fear-producing circumstances in the light of present-time adult perceptions. Most of the time, you will discover that as a capable, growth-seeking adult, the fear is a result of beliefs and experiences in the past, of a child. While the circumstances may be challenging, as a capable adult with the resources available to you to deal with them, you can proceed and accomplish something worthwhile, even amazing! And choose to feel the fear while you are accomplishing!

The beauty of training activities like the ropes course and firewalking is the conflict between the (before) belief of "I can't" and the (after) realization of the reality that "*I did*!" Such a conflict forces us to choose between these two outcomes: 1) admitting that our belief did not apply in this circumstance (and may not be relevant in many places in our adult life!) and 2) invalidating our experience (it was a fluke; it wasn't really me, it was the weather or the people I was with, etc.). That second choice allows you to Be Right about your belief, even in the face of personal evidence to the contrary! It is your choice. Which one do you habitually make?

Breaking out of the prison of fear requires that you take some risks. You must risk *feeling the fear!* If you are *willing to feel the feeling of fear,* what possibilities suddenly open up to you? Where have you avoided going or what have you avoided doing because you were unwilling to feel the feeling of fear? In fact, if you are willing to feel any feeling (say embarrassment, which is also *a major prison* and is also *inside you*), think what possibilities would open up to you!

High on the list of things people avoid is public speaking. Why? Fear of looking stupid (embarrassed) is the probable reason, driven by a childhood belief that there is something wrong with them. This is another example of the Arrogance discussed in Chapter Three. If you were willing to risk the feeling of embarrassment, some idea or contribution you could make might actually become available to humankind!

I strongly believe that when you are willing to take on a fear, or an embarrassment, and do the thing feared or that might embarrass you, over and over, until doing that thing becomes tolerable, you will discover that not only has the fear of that thing become tolerable, or the embarrassment faded, but you will also notice that the strong feelings you associate with many other things you have avoided also fade! Taking on one fear or embarrassment increases your capacity to deal with fear and embarrassment in many other areas of life. Your life will be expanded!

Look over the Life Zone Chart above and examine where you spend your life. Are you stuck in the prison of comfort zone? Or in comfort zone in some specific areas of your life? The "Edge of Your Life" is that boundary where, if you risked enough to step over it, you might discover entirely new and incredible possibilities to contribute to your own enjoyment, your family's growth and welfare, and your contribution to the world. New hobbies, new career possibilities, new creative opportunities, new ideas, new differences you can make in the world! Think of people you know or know of who stepped over that edge and changed the world forever!

Perhaps it might be useful for you to list below some things you might have done except that fear or embarrassment stopped you. Make a commitment to yourself to take on one or more and make a specific plan to do it! Then dream about what might lie outside that boundary that defines the "Edge of Your Life." What lies beyond the biggest fear you can imagine or the most embarrassing thing you can imagine doing? What lies out there beyond the biggest vision you can imagine for yourself and your life? You are a magnificent human being and won't ever in mortality fully explore your amazing potential. Most of it lies out there in that unknown place, beyond the "Edge of Your Life." Happy exploring!

-Notes to Self-

Chapter Twelve—

The Prison of Guilt and Shame

One of the tragic burdens from the past that most people carry is the burden of guilt. Like the prisons of "I Can't" and "I'm Afraid," it is a prison that keeps us locked in the past, focusing on choices and consequences in the past. "I did this awful thing."

Yes, you did. You made a mess! The mess is in the past and there it is. The past just *IS*, and nothing can be done to change it. In the present, the only value of the past is to *learn from it.*

The mess you made in the past resulted from choices you made *in the past* and those choices had consequences. No matter how painful the consequences were to you and others, nothing can be done to change the choices, nor the consequences that flowed from them. But you can learn from them. You can see patterns and habits that drove the choices. You can notice the beliefs that drove those patterns and habits. And you can work to change the beliefs and alter the patterns and habits for future choices. And in that opportunity lies the blessing of healing. If your guilt motivates you to do such introspection, it is of value. Once it has done its introspective job, it is finished and *you can let it go.* You are a better person for having made the mess *and* having learned from it. The key is *Learning From It!*

I believe that the purpose of life is to learn and grow. We come in as infants with a blank slate in front of us. We fill it with life experiences *AND* the lessons for growth that we learn from those experiences. Our life is the product of the experiences that resulted from our choices and the lessons we learned from them. I believe that every individual is worthy of life and that every life lived has the potential to learn wonderful and beautiful lessons of Empowerment from the consequences of choices made. That some do not learn, even seem committed to continuing unfortunate patterns of choice with painful or awful consequences, does not negate the sanctity of life and its magnificent potential. And this is a choice!

The journey to Empowerment therefore includes making messes *AND* doing what you can to clean them up. Sometimes the mess can be completely cleaned up. Those are easy to let go. Sometimes the consequences of our messes can't be cleaned up completely or at all. Lingering guilt may hang around from those. The key here is to acknowledge that all messes are *in the past* and once you have done all you can do or are willing to do, that is the end of the matter. The Empowered Life lives in the present. Once you have decided that no more can or will be done about a past mess, let it go and turn your vision forward

Look at yourself from the perspective of **Buffalo** in the North, from the place of having passed through the experiences of the West and learned from them. You are filled with gratitude. You see how making that mess and doing what you did to clean it up, *and* learning life lessons from it about yourself and your life patterns, all contributed to your growth. Our messes are actually blessings when we clean them up and learn from them. When we are honest with ourselves, we realize that in life we have been both perpetrators upon others and perpetrated upon by others. And since we are completely responsible for our own experience of life, we are responsible for our response to being perpetrated upon. And we are responsible for the consequences of our perpetrations.

If this seems like a guilt-producing paradox, it may be a good place to pause and contemplate this precious idea: ***Everyone is responsible and no one is to blame!* Messes happen. People make them. Pain and suffering are a consequence. Empowered people do what they can to clean up their messes, alleviate the pain and suffering as much as possible, and move on. Everyone is responsible for their own life experience and dealing with the lingering consequences of all messes from the past. *Blame is irrelevant to the Empowered!***

What about shame? Guilt results from the perception that I did something bad. Shame is a terrible burden from the past and results from the perception that *I AM BAD*. It is the on-going legacy of the infant's conclusion that "There is something wrong with me; I'm not

OK!" It is the continuing confirmation of that conclusion as perceived through the messes made. It is Being Right about one's beliefs about one being *Not* OK. It is the driving force behind low self-esteem and victimhood. It is the basis for a *disempowered* Belief System. Because it lies at the core of one's very perception of reality, and self in reality, and is the filter through which one perceives everything about one's life including self, it is difficult to root out. It is the focus of **Owl's** work with us.

Unless you are willing to challenge that very foundation of your beliefs about yourself, you have condemned yourself to a life sentence in the Prison of Shame. But there is a way out. It requires putting your adult mind in charge of your life and recognizing that Being Right about these old beliefs is just a habit. It requires that you realize that your belief system is simply the result of choices you made and conclusions you drew as an infant and young child. It requires that you look in the present for the evidence upon which to base your choices. It requires that you build a new habit of choosing *based in the present*. And it requires that you surround yourself with a support circle of others who see your magnificence and your OK-ness and will continue to affirm it to you as you build your new habit of belief in yourself.

I can't emphasize enough that the Empowered Life *is rooted in the Present*. The past *JUST IS* and from the present perspective, only has value in the lessons that can be learned from it. Guilt and shame draw their power over our lives from the past. They lose their power over us when we live our lives in the present with our attention focused on who we really are and what we want. Be-Do-Have.

Perhaps you might find it useful to list below some things about which you harbor feelings of guilt. Note that the choices you made to produce the messes were all made in the past *and can't be changed*. With each item, list what you have already done to clean up the mess *and* what you might still do to clean it up more. Make a commitment to do those things. Check off those items about which you have already done all that you can or are willing to do; they are candidates for letting go. Then make an adult decision to actually let them go and move on. This is an ongoing process in the Empowered Life. We are never done with making messes and cleaning them up! Remember, *I'm OK! I'm Just Not finished!*

Are you living in a Prison of Shame? Do you have underlying feelings of unworthiness? Feelings that no one, not even God can accept you as you are? Perhaps you might find it useful to examine your circle of friends and approach some trusted ones for feedback about the truth of your magnificence. (The next chapter is about feedback). Remember Unconditional Love of Self. It might be time to seek professional support from a facilitator or counselor to bring your paradigm up to date for the adult you are.

-Notes to Self-

Chapter Thirteen—

Feedback, the Life Blood of Champions

There is a heartwarming Olympics story that illustrates many wonderful things. I will tell it all, then use it to illustrate an important principle, the importance of Feedback to the Empowered Life. For context, here is the whole story.

Back in the 1992 Summer Olympics at Barcelona, Spain, a group of young girls competed in women's gymnastics. I'm sure this drama plays out in some form at every Olympics, because women's gymnastics has become a sport mostly for young girls. At these particular games there was a young teenager on the USA team named Kim Zmeskal. She had for her coach Bela Karolyi, who was world known as the coach of Nadia Comaneci. Now Nadia was the first woman in Olympic gymnastics history to score perfect tens. At Nadia's time, individual scores were written on cards and held up for the judges, the audience and the competitors to see. The scores were written on the cards with one decimal place.

Kim Zmeskal started her journey to the world stage of gymnastics when she was very young. At the age of six, her family enrolled her in a run-down gymnastics studio just bought by Karolyi in Houston, Texas. For her to have committed to achieve a place on the United States Women's Gymnastics Team would have required *her* to decide at a very early age to commit *herself* to *whatever it takes* to get there. Her mother's or father's commitment would, by itself, not have taken her to that world class arena. The day that Kim Zmeskal decided *She* was committed to championship, she became a champion!

Bela Karolyi was her coach. She wanted the very best. I'm sure he did not come cheap. For him to agree to be her personal coach and for her family and supporters to agree to pay his fee required some serious commitment. Kim's time with Karolyi was very precious, too precious to waste. Minute by minute, time was too precious to waste!

Now (and we are getting to the point) what did Kim Zmeskal most want from her coach? By the time Kim was entering serious competition, scores were being tallied by computer and reported to the second decimal place. The difference between the gold and silver medals in world-class competition was often *in the second decimal place!* Out in the hundredths of a point. If Kim wanted to compete in that arena, she needed to hone her performance to a sharpness never before achieved, and to compete with the other world class young gymnasts working around the world, to a sharp edge out in the second decimal place. She needed from her coach absolutely truthful and pointed correction to her every move and routine. She needed *Feedback;* pointed, ruthless, perhaps brutal feedback. Time was too precious to waste on glad-talk. The only value she would have placed on positive commentary was to draw her attention to something that worked well that she might not have noticed and needed to consciously refine into her performance.

At the Olympics, the TV color commentator told the worldwide audience how often in practice, Kim—as a young woman at puberty—would leave the session in tears because the emotional intensity was so great for her young years. But she had hired the best coach she could find to perfect her performance for the Olympics arena and she was committed to compete in that arena. She would quickly compose herself and return in a few minutes to continue the relentless honing of a true champion.

An incredible moment in the 1992 Summer Olympics came on the balance beam. Kim mounted the beam and began her routine. The TV camera focused in on her. The commentator noted the movements of her routine. The entire world was watching. Then. . . .she fell off the beam!

The commentator gasped, and in that gasp broadcast around the world, one could almost hear the entire world gasp! The commentator then said that mistake would probably cost her not only a medal in this individual event, but also a chance to be in the all-around competition. The camera cut to Karolyi, and even he remarked that her chances were remote. The next moment was the defining moment, a sign of the true champion. Kim Zmeskal got up off the floor, remounted the beam, and in front of the entire world, finished her routine. She continued with the competition and amazingly did achieve a place in the all-around competition. I will always remember Kim Zmeskal, not for medals, for she did not win any individual medal that I can recall, and I have forgotten the names of every medal winner anyway.

I will always remember Kim Zmeskal for showing me true championship and the spirit of Whatever It Takes. I'll never know what was in her heart as she watched the cherished medals go to others. I do know *she made a difference in my life* that day with her demonstration of determination to finish the course as the champion she was. And as you ponder her story, *perhaps a difference in yours.*

Among the many things illustrated by this story, the point I want to make is the importance of Feedback. Feedback is the lifeblood of growth and progress for the Empowered Life. Feedback is information about how we are perceived, how we are doing in the experience of others. The champion seeks it; the sandlot players hide from it. The Empowered Life thrives on it; the disempowered victim fears it and avoids it, both in giving it and receiving it.

In that regard, if you are about to go out and meet your public (whatever your public is in any area or any moment of your life) and your fly is open, what do you most want from your colleagues? *Tell you* for crying out loud! And what are your colleagues most likely to do? Not tell you! And this because of embarrassment or fear of *hurting your feelings.*

So you go out and meet your public. Does your public notice your fly is open? *Of course!* And it may affect your results with them. When you get back to your colleagues, how do you feel? You turkeys! You let me go out there knowing that my fly was open and *you didn't tell me!*

Take a look at those areas of your life where reside important parts of what you want. Is it possible that you have some flies open in some of those areas? Some skills that need honing, some things that need learning, some habits to alter, some beliefs or attitudes that might get in the way of your results? Professional flies, personal flies, relationship flies, spiritual flies. And would it improve your likelihood of getting what you want if you could correct those open flies? Would the information that others might share, who know you and care about you, be of value to you in fixing those open flies? Who would you go to for the best or most useful information? Your spouse, your child, your coworker, your boss, your employee, your neighbor, your friend, a customer, a competitor? Who?

Remember The Box back in Chapter One? Did you notice that label on the box? Did you notice where it is? It's on the *outside of the box!* Who can't see it? You can't! Who can see it? Everyone else!

That label contains the directions for *how to get out of your box.*

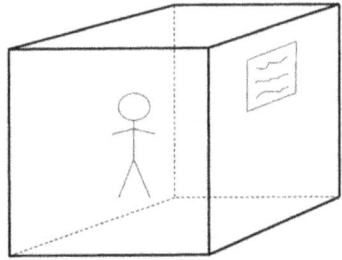

You see, your box, your paradigm of perceptions—the filter that transforms what is real into your perception of it—is self-contained. It is difficult for you to find your own way out from inside your box. You will spend all of your life imprisoned in your box of perceptions. It is what reality looks like to you. You will never see beyond your own perceptions for they *are* what registers in your conscious mind through all your filters. You might work on the filters, even change them, but your filters, represented by your Belief System, are always between you and what is real.

However, *others* can see your label. Others are not inside your box. They are inside theirs, but not yours. Others can see you from outside your box. The information on that label is what we call feedback! Others can see your open flies. Others can also see your magnificence. Others can give you information about yourself that you will not see looking at the perception of you reflected back on the inside of your box. Feedback may be the most valuable information available to you on your Journey of Empowerment!

First, here are some types of communication that often *disguise* as feedback.

1. **Judgment:** valuable feedback is not judgment. It has nothing to do with who you are or your worth as a human being or

judgments about the goodness or badness of your behaviors. No matter who it comes from, judgment is not feedback.

2. **Criticism:** valuable feedback is not criticism. It is not offered to correct anything nor does it come with threats or energy.
3. **Advice:** valuable feedback is not advice. It does not come with strings attached or expectations that it will be adopted.

Now for what true and useful Feedback *is!*
1. Feedback is honest, truthful and direct, no glad talk.
2. Feedback is based on *my* experience of you; it is *my perception* and *I* own it.
3. Feedback is given unconditionally, no strings attached, without any expectations that you will do anything with it or even that you will receive it.
4. Feedback is given because *I care enough about you* to be honest.
5. Feedback is most beneficial when it is requested.

The Empowered Life seeks sources of useful information. Once the Feedback session is engaged, honest feedback is requested. Demonstration of a sincere desire for useful Feedback might be having a notebook and pencil to take notes and using them during the conversation. Ask clarifying questions to penetrate deeper into useful areas; this shows your source your sincere interest to honestly and boldly give you the information you seek. If you detect a reluctance to be direct and forthright, give continuing encouragement and assurance to your source that you really want honest information. You have come to this person because you feel they are familiar enough with you in this particular area of your life to give you useful information and you believe they care enough about you to be honest and forthright. Let them know. You may well be asking that person to take some considerable risks and he/she might well feel quite uncomfortable with the level of honesty you seek and that will be useful to you!

When the Feedback session is complete, the only appropriate response to true Feedback is of the form, "Thank you." "Thank you for caring

enough about me to be honest." "I appreciate your willingness to take a risk and share your experience of me in these important areas." With true Feedback, you are under no obligation to do anything with it. It is simply information. If it is useful, put it to work. Deal with the issues that are identified. And let your provider know how valuable it is. And especially, if you value the feedback, let your provider see the results show up in your life for him or her having risked giving Feedback to you. Remember **Buffalo** and the Principle of Gratitude.

Are you ready to risk seeking some Feedback now? Try your spouse, or your child, or your sibling, or your boss, or your parent. Seeking and using Feedback accelerates your Empowered Life process!

Remember, there is no "good" or "bad" news, *there is only news.* You decide whether any particular news is good or bad. Why not decide that everything is good news, *even the stuff thrown at you as judgment or criticism?* Whoa! Why not simply choose to perceive all of it as information and respond to the thrower with, "Thank you for sharing." Remember others only behave; you always choose how you respond!

Isn't it amazing how *your choices and decisions* about your perceptions determine how you experience them and respond to them! *You get this simple principle and your relationships will change!* Your entire experience of life will change!

Ahh, Empowerment! The power of choices and options! The power of being free to choose my response!

Perhaps it might be useful to list below some candidates from whom you can gain good feedback about open flies in important areas of your life. When will you ask them to provide it?

-Notes to Self-

Section Four—
Empowered Relationships

Chapter Fourteen—
You, Me, Us

Reality, as we perceive and experience it, is a complex of things, people and concepts. Everything in reality has a place or slot in your perception. Every tree, plant, bug, person, action, behavior, circumstance, everything we perceive and experience has a slot and a title/name in our reality. Around each slot is a set of beliefs and expectations that define it, its meaning, and its role in our life experience, and a title. Some of our beliefs and expectations may have strong emotional charge associated with them. When those beliefs and expectations are challenged or violated, we may experience strong feelings and upset in our life. **Owl** is visiting!

We begin structuring our reality early in the womb. From conception through the first few weeks or months of mortal existence outside the womb, our reality consists of basically one slot, *Me*. During the early part of our life in the womb, we begin to experience something outside of our self, through sound vibrations, our mother's movements, our mother's emotions in their raw chemical form from the chemicals of feelings that course through her bloodstream and cross the placenta. We do not have an experiential context to give meaning to these feelings, but we experience a chemical shot of the feelings none-the-less.

At birth, we *gradually* begin to have direct experience of another slot in our reality, *Non-Me*. Beliefs and expectations begin to form as we enlarge and adapt our reality to this new, emerging two-slotted experience. (Keep in mind that these beliefs are not in our Cognitive Mind, for that is not yet developed, but in the Affective Mind.) Early in life, non-me begins to subdivide into separate slots—mom, dad, siblings, family, non-family, and on and on. Slots for boy and girl separate from each other with sets of beliefs and expectations associated with each.

At a magical time associated with puberty, boy/girl becomes further subdivided along romantic and sexual lines and we have boy vs. boyfriend and girl vs. girlfriend. These evolve further with hormonal growth into romantic and sexual partner with a complex set of beliefs and expectations around those. Somewhere in late teen/young adulthood, slots for committed relationship and spouse begin to be defined. Two separate perceptions of reality come together into a single context that involves two individual realities, mostly unknown to the other, and with subconscious parts largely unknown even to self. A relationship is born. Now the stage is set for **Owl** to *really go to work.*

In every relationship between two people there actually exists the possibility for three entities: You, Me, and Us. Many relationships are formed around only two of these, you and me. In such relationships, each member is only in so far. Commitment is conditional. Something like "50:50" is the tone of things. There is not enough confidence in the relationship to motivate either partner to not keep a back door open for possible escape. Risking and vulnerability are minimized. The relationship contains a large component of "I'll be darned if I'm going to get hurt again!"

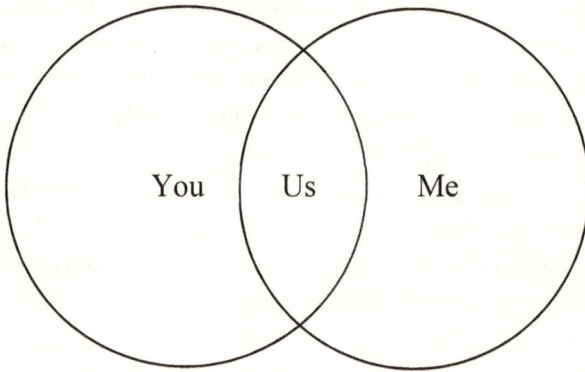

In truly committed relationships, confidence drives a willingness to be vulnerable. Emotional risks are taken. The spirit of 100% commitment and Whatever-It-Takes gives energy and vitality to the relationship. A *third entity* comes into being, *an actual entity* in the Universe, *Us.* Thus in a truly committed relationship there exists three entities, You, Me, *and Us.* Us cannot exist without both You and Me present and fully committed.

It is possible in committed relationships for an unhealthy situation to arise. In such an unhealthy state, the focus is on Us to the exclusion of You and Me. This might be referred to as enmeshment. It is important to realize that no matter how committed the relationship, there are two different people involved. No matter how compatible and committed to each other, each person has unique personal perceptions, needs and nourishments that are not completely shared. This unhealthy state of enmeshment might develop when either partner feels jealous of time the other spends alone, with hobbies, or with outside friends and interests. Expressions of anger or resentment over such matters may be a sign that too much attention is being focused on Us and not enough consideration is being given to You and Me.

In a healthy committed relationship, attention is given to the individual needs and interests of each partner, the You and the Me, as well as the common aspects of Us. There is explicit or implicit encouragement for each partner to pursue personal needs and interests. Time and resources are allocated by the pair for each to use for personal purposes. Confidence and trust in the relationship are sufficient that to develop self is not perceived as a threat to the other or to the relationship as a whole.

In committed relationships such as marriage, there are three forms they may take. In many world cultures, especially our Western culture and many of its religious communities, a form of relationship called Patriarchy is promoted. In Patriarchy, the male figure has the dominant role and is considered Head of the House. In this role, final authority resides in the Patriarch.

The second and similar form, Matriarchy, is rarer in public acknowledgment, but often shows up in the closet. So we often think of relationship as either one or the other. And many of the models we have to follow, parents, grandparents, prominent figures, seem to be one or the other. It is either-or as far as relationship is concerned.

There is a third form of relationship. I call it *Partnership*. In Partnership there is no head of the house. Two people of different physical and emotional makeup each view the other as equal. *Equality is in the Being of the relationship, not in the Doing or Having.* Agreed on and different "doing" roles may be assigned. But decisions are shared and are reached by consensus (discussed in Chapter 1). In true Partnership consensus, both must agree or there is no decision. Communication continues in Partnership until an outcome evolves which is satisfying to both partners, consensus. True Partnership requires a high degree of communication and a mutual willingness and commitment to achieve such outcomes. Vulnerability and risking are maximized. Commitment is at 100% levels. There are no back doors.

The rewards of personal and partnership growth are immense. I believe that in Partnership the Empowered Life has its greatest opportunities for challenge and growth, and its greatest opportunities for expression and achievement. And in Partnership, I believe the fruits of **Owl** work have their most marvelous opportunity to be realized!

I discovered something later in life. I wish it had come earlier; my life would have played out much differently had I been paying attention to this as a young man. Unfortunately, as teenagers and young adults, most of us are too engaged in hormones to pay much attention to this very important reality. But here it is.

In picking partners for relationship, what you see is what you get (WYSIWYG)!

What this means is very simple and so easy to lose in the flood of hormones that in our youth we call "love" and, as a society, we have come to believe form the primary basis of relationship.

What you see is what you get. All the stuff that irritates you, that alarms you, that disgusts you; all that stuff that seriously bugs you (come on, get out of denial, *you see it!*) **plus** a whole lot more that *you haven't seen yet*, **You Get!** It comes with the complete package of the other person. You get it all!

If you happen to be right now in that wonderful experience of "falling in love," and are head over heels infatuated with that other, wonderful person, and are blinded by your own infatuation from the things about that other person that irritate and annoy you, and believe that in coming together in consummation of that love the other will surely change and not annoy you, I invite you to pay very close attention to this part of this book, especially the next bolded paragraph.

The Empowered Life <u>does not expect</u> the other to change anything, *ever*. The other person *owes you nothing*. The Empowered Life accepts complete responsibility for itself and its own happiness. The Empowered Life does not enter into relationship with the *hope* that anything seen will ever change or the *expectation* that, surely it will change. WYSIWYG applies forever! If you can't accept that principle, if there is *anything* in the other person that you *cannot accept forever* without any expectation that change will ever occur, *then don't get into the relationship!* No matter what hormonal involvement you have. *Remember that love is NOT reason enough to get married!*

Failure to get this principle is a sure set-up for upset and sadness in relationship. It is an invitation to ultimate victimhood and misery. You cannot change another person. Change is initiated from within. And your expectation or eventual insistence that your partner will change is a recipe for eventual unhappiness, or dissolution of the relationship. *Expectations are premeditated disappointments!* Expectations are how we hold someone hostage to our will, and which denies them choice regarding how they want to show up on the planet or in a relationship. *Agreements* are much better than expectations. Expectations only create distance, and are ways we make others wrong. Expectations are how we intentionally choose to avoid closeness or intimacy.

Perhaps it might be useful for you to evaluate your relationships, especially your primary ones (parents, spouse, children, in-laws), and write below what you notice. What form do they take (Patriarchal, Matriarchal, Partnership)? How is the balance among You, Me, and Us? How are you doing with respect to accepting your partner? What is particularly annoying about your partner? What expectations or hopes do you have about your partner changing anything? How do the things you notice relate to the degree of fulfillment and happiness each person seems to experience?

-Notes to Self-

Chapter Fifteen—

Who Is Right?

Empowered Individuals build Empowered Relationships. The question, What do I want? expands to include and embrace, What do *We* want? The Empowered Partnership relationship is founded on total ownership of one's own life by each partner *and* total ownership of *the Partnership* by each partner. In such a context the following statement makes sense:

For two people to be together,
they don't have to agree on what's right;
they just have to want to be together.

If that sounds simple, try it sometime.

> — adapted from Paul Williams
> in Das Energi (Elektra Records, 1973)

Empowered Individuals realize that *both are right*, all the time! They realize that both live in a box, each in his/her individual box, and each filters reality through a unique subconscious filter, unknowable by the other, and largely unknown even to self. And perceived through this filter, each is Right in his/her perception!

Truth vs. Perception Of Truth

Remember Chapter 1? Let's review. As human beings we have only five physical ways to perceive the world, our five physical senses. These are our only mechanisms for input from the physical world and our life in it. Sight, hearing, touch, smell, and taste. That's it! OK, we might add to these five that "sixth" intuitive or inner sense, *also a perceptual sense for it also passes through the filter of our Belief System.*

These six mechanisms are *our only ways to perceive anything*. *Everything* that we perceive comes to our core of consciousness through one or more of these perceptual senses. That's it! Period! As far as your life experience is concerned, *you don't know what is real!* You only know what you *perceive* to be real. **Maybe you ought to pause again and let that soak in a bit,** *in the context of relationship.* This realization is critical in an Empowered Relationship. As far as your life experience is concerned, and especially your experience in relationship, you don't know what is real. You only know what you *perceive to be real!*

This Reality that we perceive is *filtered* through our Paradigm. Our Paradigm is the sum total of our conclusions (drawn since infancy) about how the world is and how we are in it. It is our complete Belief System. It is our personal definition of our individual reality. It is our conclusions about what is Supposed To Be. Our Belief System, our Paradigm, *IS* our *total inner Definition of Reality*. Somewhere down at the core of your soul, where your being-ness resides, is where you perceive from, through the filter of your beliefs. So all of your perceptions, of self, of others, of events, of circumstances, of all the things in your world and in your experience, are filtered through your beliefs about everything. I cannot emphasize this enough! If you don't yet *Get This*, you should spend some time right here pondering it. If you don't *Get It*, the fundamental message of this book won't really make much sense or be of maximum value to you.

We *perceive* Reality as we *believe* Reality to be. We literally create our own perceived Reality through our conclusions and beliefs about it. This is sometimes called the law of attraction—we attract what we believe and that belief is then affirmed. For the disempowered victims of the world, how they view Reality *IS* how Reality is for them, period! And they are Right! (Unless, of course, they are willing to change the filter!)

This applies to all of us, and in the world of relationship and of personal growth, *especially to all of us*. We have conflicts in our relationships because our perceptions of life and circumstances in it and our perceptions of each other are different. *We argue and fight because the other perceives me differently than I perceive myself or perceives things in the world differently than I perceive them.* I insist that my perception is "right" and the perceptions of the other person are "wrong," because that is how I see things. Surely everyone sees reality like I see it. After all, it is what I see!

How much of our life energy do we spend trying to convince one another that we are right and they are wrong—*or even sometimes trying to convince ourselves?*

Pause and let this idea soak in:

We Can Either Be Right,
***Or* We Can Have Relationship.**
We Can Rarely Have Both!

Every person's perception is "right" according to his/her definition of Reality (Paradigm). Therefore *no one* can tell another that his or her perception is wrong! It *IS* their perception! Honesty in language therefore requires that we stop telling another how they are "supposed to" perceive something or that they are "wrong" in their perception of something. We can only express how *We* perceive something, ask clarifying questions about the other's expression of their perception so that we can be as clear in our understanding as possible of what each other's perception is, and discuss the differences. *Until we truly get this*, we are unable to have meaningful dialogue to resolve differences without power struggles, fighting over who is right, or one or both parties "selling out" to achieve some "perceived resolution." **Selling Out Is Not Resolution!**

Resolution comes from genuine acceptance of the outcome. Whenever there is sell-out, anger, resentment, and incompleteness remain *and there is no real resolution.* There is a lot of meat here! Pause and ponder. It can change your life! *How many times have you given yourself away and not stood in your truth in order to be accepted or approved by someone?* Win/win is the only *REAL* outcome. That is the law of the universe.

When we truly get this fundamental principle about perception and extend it throughout our life, we realize that there is no such thing as "Truth" as far as our life experience is concerned. There is only our *"perception of truth!"* Therefore it is entirely possible (in fact *most probable!*) that *no* two people will agree entirely on what "Truth" is! Even at the level of little details of what is perceived!

We can both look at the exact same thing (from our individual perspective) and perceive it differently! We are both Right, in our perception! All the time! Every time! That includes "Truth" about ourselves as well as "Truth" about the other person, and "Truth" about the Universe—until we realize it isn't actually Truth, only our Perception of Truth. Even if we work to change it—even after we change it—it is still only our perception of Truth!

Hello out there! Hello to you who tell me you have the Truth, the only Truth, and that I must accept your Truth. Hello to you who say that if I don't accept your Truth, I am unacceptable, to you, to your culture, to God. Hello to you who insist that if I don't accept your Truth about how life should be lived and how I should behave, I am not OK—even inferior.

I perceive myself, my statements, my behaviors, my attitudes, and everything about me, through my Paradigm filter about how I believe myself to be in my Reality. Someone else perceives me through their paradigm filter about how I am *in the role I fill in **his/her** Reality.* Those two perceptions are very unlikely to be the same, possibly not even close! The value of realizing and owning this principle is that I no longer need to be defensive or argue "rightness" about my perception against another. I can simply state my perception, listen, and learn from theirs. If the issue being perceived is critical to the relationship, then we can discuss the differences with the hope of achieving mutual understanding, perhaps some shift in perception, and/or some mutually acceptable conclusion. Failing that (if we truly live the principle), *we can agree to disagree, or we can terminate the relationship.* Those are our options. Period! Shift of perceptions, acceptance of different perceptions, or separation. Of course, another option is continuing strife over who is right, and ongoing misery (victimhood!). And we always have the power to choose among our options, *or life will choose them for us and we get them by default!* Proactive choice, or choice by default.

Based on the principle that we only *perceive* Truth, the realization that there is no such thing as Truth as far as our life experience is concerned produces an enormous shift in Paradigm. We can thereafter live respectfully in a world of diversity, sharing our perceptions and experiences, listening and learning as others share their perceptions and experiences. We can relate with those we want to relate to, without requiring that they change anything or emulate us in order to validate us. We can listen to another's perception of us as honest feedback, nothing to defend against, and look at possible applications to ourselves. We can look for patterns in the feedback. We can look at the results we perceive in our own life and look for patterns there. Who knows, we might learn something that *WE* can apply to change our own experience of life! We can offer to another, in the spirit of love and caring, our honest perceptions and experience of them simply as information they might find useful. All of this as commentary, not as superior judgment, criticism, or advice, with no requirement that they do anything with what we shared. Life becomes an opportunity to learn, grow, and share with each other. True Partnership!

For two people to be together, they don't have to agree on what's right. In fact, it is almost guaranteed they *won't* agree on what's right all the time! Maybe won't even frequently agree on what's right! All that is required is that they want to be together. And if that is what they want, what price are they willing to pay to have that, to have relationship? How about WIT, whatever it takes! If both are willing to do whatever it takes, then dealing with differences comes along with the territory. The issue is *NOT* who is right or who has the power. The issue is: when we don't see things the same *and* a decision has to be made or an outcome needs to be derived, we must stay in communication and develop mechanisms to make decisions with which both of us can be satisfied. Dealing with differences provides another opportunity for Empowered Individuals to grow and learn. What is right *for US* is better than who is right *among us*. Ain't life great!

This is important enough to get again! The issue is *NOT* who is right or who has the power. The issue is: **When we don't see things the same *and* a decision has to be made, we need to develop mechanisms in our relationship by which we can make decisions**

with which we can both be satisfied—without selling out and giving ourselves away. You recognize when sell-out happens because you failed to stand in your truth and you feel regretful and resentful. The conversation in your head about the situation continues. You gave away your truth to avoid judgment, loss, or retribution. This is not power. This is not relationship. One of you played small so the other could play big. That is Patriarchy or Matriarchy, not Partnership!

Did you get it? Your life and your relationships will change if you did!

Perhaps you might find it useful to introspect here and honestly write down how important it is for you to "be right" about things in your relationships. And then get real by writing the results that you actually experience in these relationships because of this insistence. Are those the results that you really want? Be honest with yourself. Denial gets you the booby prize! What price do you pay for Being Right? What would happen to your relationships if you recognized that the other person is also right? What would happen to your world and your place in it if you turned more of your attention to listening and learning from others and less to defending and promoting your own perceptions? It's your life, and you only have one opportunity to live it.

-Notes to Self-

Chapter Sixteen—

Is it OK with Us that You bother Me sometimes?

Since it is almost impossible that any two of us are going to agree all the time on what's right, it is inevitable that you are going to violate my expectations and beliefs around the role you fill in my Reality now and then. In fact maybe more now than then! So in my Empowered Life and in our Empowered Relationship, I get to accept that you are going to bother me sometimes. In our relationship, let's acknowledge that fact up front and develop some skills and mechanisms to deal with it in an empowered, resourceful way.

In an Empowered Relationship, there are three things for me to realize, acknowledge, and reinforce about being bothered by you sometimes. *One,* I have already decided that I am completely and totally responsible for my own experience of life, period. *Two,* I already know and accept that any time something outside of me triggers some reaction within me, *it is my issue* and an opportunity for me to learn something about myself and grow a bit. I am not a victim of you and I am not a victim of myself. I am living an accountable, Empowered Life and seek learning and growth. *Three,* being in relationship with you *is more important to me* than Being Right about what is bothering me. This requires that I be clear on my priorities! *Let that last one soak in!*

From these three realizations, a simple tool can be employed in a committed Empowered Relationship. This simple tool can be employed to eliminate conflict and reduce the amount of time and energy either or both of the partners spend being bothered, turning bother into an opportunity for reinforcement of the basis of the relationship and into learning and growth. I call this tool The Conflict Dialogue. Both of you need to memorize it and post it on the fridge for easy reference. I like the word "triggered" to express that one is being bothered. If you have a better word, feel free to use it.

The Conflict Dialogue

The Underlying Principles of The Dialogue—When conflicts arise, leading to strong feelings (perhaps anger and blaming):

- Acknowledge it.
- Own it.
- Deal with it as a *personal issue* of self-discovery and growth.
- *Then* resolve any differences based on honoring personal truth *and* being clear on priorities (e.g., placing *higher value* on the relationship than on Being Right).

The Conflict Dialogue—Memorize it, and deliver it exactly!

1. *"I'm triggered."* (The signal to your partner that a critical moment has been entered)
2. *"and the thing that triggers me is my perception that. . . ."* (Describe the behavior, incident, or circumstance that triggers you. Keep it in accountable terms! Own it as '**my perception!**')
3. *"and I know my being triggered has nothing to do with you"* (this is the <u>critical statement of ownership</u>! Your partner's behavior may have been a triggering influence, but among available options, *you chose* to be triggered!)
4. *"and if this interaction continues in this triggered state, it is likely to go in a direction I don't want to go with you because I value you and I value this relationship too much."*
5. *"Therefore I need to withdraw for a while*
   a. *to get out of the triggered state I'm in, and*
   b. *to see if I can discover what it is about me such that this triggers me so much."* (You see, if you were **unconditionally accepting of yourself and your partner**, you would be emotionally **neutral** about this circumstance. That there is emotional charge is an invitation to examine *your* beliefs and *your* expectations. **Bear** is calling you into the cave for some introspection!)

Note: this dialogue presumes that two people *of good will* are involved who are willing to accept responsibility for their lives. It won't work in a seriously codependent setting (see the next chapters) or in one where there is mental or emotional illness or intent to hurt or do damage. If such is the case, get professional help!

There are a few ground rules that go along with using this dialogue.

1. No one can point to the fridge and say to the other, "Hey, you are not following the dialogue!" Or "You need to be using the dialogue!" Watch out for that word "you!"
2. In fact, no one can point anywhere but to self in any regard while using the dialogue.
3. The dialogue is voluntary and should be initiated *by the person who is bothered.* The one who is causing the bother has no business referring to the dialogue.
4. If *patterns of causing bother* can be identified <u>by the one causing the bother</u>, it might be empowering to the relationship for that person to look at these patterns and take them on as a personal growth opportunity, while the other one is off learning about why the bother is so triggering! Partnership is about US. **Bear** works with both partners!

I am a believer that in an Empowered Relationship, setting some ground rules is useful and productive. These are openly discussed and should include mutually acceptable mechanisms for making decisions when both partners don't see things the same way. Good ground rules can include anything that the two partners feel is important to their relationship and should also include provisions for amending and adding to them as the relationship grows and progresses (which an Empowered Relationship will!). The ground rules are a set of relationship bylaws. Perhaps they should be written down and posted on the fridge alongside The Conflict Dialogue.

Now, that's all well and good, but even Empowered Individuals are human, right? Right! *If you catch yourself triggering another, you can stop at any time. You are not a victim of yourself. You are at choice, unless you are running a reactionary pattern of behavior. Pay attention to the patterns!*

Agreeing To The Rules

In Partnership relationships, there is no 'top dog' or 'head of the house;' therefore all decisions are subject to consensus, consensus being defined in Partnership as continuing with the communication until an outcome evolves with which both partners are satisfied (see Chapter 1). The 'rules of the game' need to be defined, by consensus. Consensus says, "We are both in to the outcome (not necessarily for the same reasons)." If the partners are not both in, there is no consensus! Like conflict resolution, consensus building is a skill that can be learned. In Chapter 1, the "Talking Feather" technique is presented for achieving consensus. If there is concern that understanding of the agreed rules may be fuzzy, discuss them, *write them down*, and both "sign and date" them.

What happens, then, when one of the partners violates the rules in the perception of the other?

Here are the available options to the Partnership:

1. Restate the rules for clarity. Clear up any misunderstandings (refer to the written rules, if necessary) and recommit, a new "sign and date."
2. The partners can change or amend the old rules by new consensus.
3. The partners can define new rules by consensus.
4. One or both partners can choose *Not To Play* anymore (this has pretty serious consequences, leading to dissolution of the partnership!).

Or

5. One partner can "sell-out" to the other, or give in, or go off sulking, or even worse, retreat into the ice treatment. The consequence of this will be silent resentment, ultimately a

cancer to the relationship. This is not a direction leading to empowerment and may have the same ultimate result as choosing *Not To Play*! This is victimology.

In the world of the Inner-Directed Life, option four, choosing not to play anymore, *IS* an acceptable option. Only in the world of Supposed To, are couples expected to stay together, come hell or high water, in misery and conflict, "until death do us part." Empowered Individuals would see bagging the relationship as a last resort—but in a world of What-Do-I-Want?—it is possible for two people's deepest wants to be incompatible. Sometimes people must get real with themselves and each other and admit that Whatever-It-Takes to preserve a destructive situation is honestly too high a price. In that case, not playing anymore is a *very kind and caring conclusion*. My former wife of thirty years and I came to that conclusion and we parted amiably. That was also the case with my **Owl** companion. We decided not to play anymore and we parted friends.

One of the greatest decisions an Empowered Relationship can make is to pay attention to the details where the two realities rub together. Some might term this "the small stuff" as in "Don't sweat the small stuff." Perhaps good advice, but *bad advice* if interpreted as "ignore the small stuff." It is in the details of daily living, the proverbial "squeezing the tooth paste tube" stuff, that the fabric of the relationship has its opportunities for real empowerment and growth. It is here that the greatest opportunities to create and work out true partnership are found. This is where we create mechanisms to make meaningful decisions when we don't see reality the same *and the stakes are relatively low*. This is where we deal with the details of sharing a common space and an overlapping life called *US*, when our basic assumptions about life and its details are different and sometimes (perhaps often?) conflict, *and we can work out our mechanisms where the consequences are relatively low*.

Remember, for two people to be together, they don't have to agree on what is right. They just have to want to be together. _If that sounds simple, try it sometime!_

Perhaps it might be useful for you to think of some recent times when conflicts have arisen in your relationships and write the results you noticed. How much energy was expended in arguing over differences in perception? How could the results have been different if the energy had been expended on listening and learning about the other person's way of perceiving? How could the results have been different if the energy had been expended on taking on some personal growth issues illuminated by the conflicts? Write down your commitment to sharing The Conflict Dialogue with your partner and working out some ground rules for applying and using it. List some situations where paying attention to the details, "the small stuff," provides you and your partner with wonderful opportunities to work out decision-making mechanisms *AND* while you are at it, laugh with **Coyote** about life!

-Notes to Self-

Chapter Seventeen—

Codependence

A healthy psyche can be diagramed as a solid circle. The circle represents clear boundaries around a life zone we can identify as the zone of choice. Within those clear boundaries is an Empowered Life, responsible for its choices and their consequences. The circumstances that present themselves to that Empowered Life are outside of those boundaries. ***Empowerment is the decision the individual makes to remain at choice with respect to all circumstances***, free to choose a resourceful response among the options that can be seen. Life energy is expended at the will and choice of the individual. "I am in charge of my life and nothing gets through my boundaries unless I choose to let it in!"

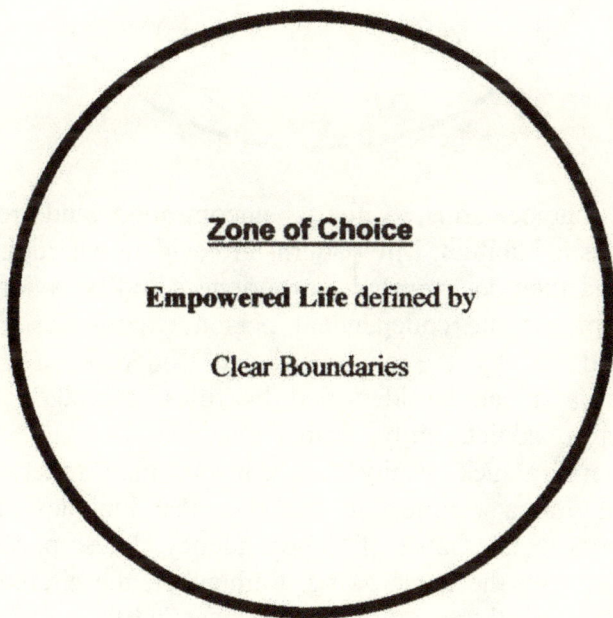

<u>**Zone of Choice**</u>

Empowered Life defined by

Clear Boundaries

Codependence can be diagramed as a leaky circle. Boundaries are not clear or are non-existent. Little or no choice is perceived to exist

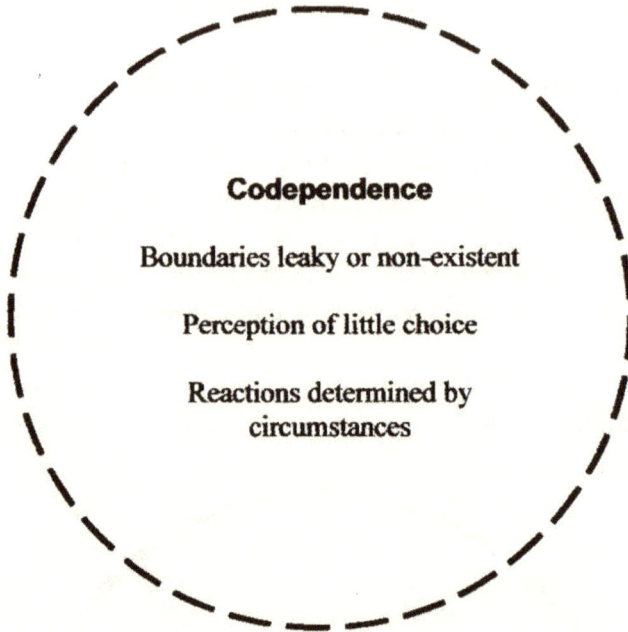

Codependence

Boundaries leaky or non-existent

Perception of little choice

Reactions determined by
circumstances

within the choice zone. Life is uncontrolled and reaction to circumstances is habitual. Life patterns are evident. Circumstances are in control and they determine life experiences and behaviors. Lack of boundaries means the codependent person experiences life energy being sucked out by the circumstances. Codependent dramas are stereotypical and can be identified by titles: caretaker, controller, whiner, victim, addict, bully, drama queen or drama king, abuser, crybaby, attention suck, vanity queen, macho man, hider, etc. Every codependent drama requires *an audience* that includes at least the other player(s) in the Game of Codependency. These players are the Enablers that keep the game going. Remember, the circumstances of life include all the other people we experience in life.

I believe most relationships between "normal" people have some elements of Codependence and therefore provide great opportunities for growth and personal development. I present Codependency in outline form, as a series of steps, for a simple way to understand the sequential process by which Codependency arises as a <u>strategy of living</u> (refer to *How I Set Up My Life and Paradigm* in Chapter Two). Understanding how codependence arises through decisions made as a child is **Wolf** teaching us of causes and effects in our lives.

1. Each of us is born into a world that may or may not "make sense" (i.e., it may or may not be consistent and predictable). Most of us find the world *doesn't make sense* (i.e., it is inconsistent and unpredictable, even under the best of circumstances). In that "normal" world that most of us encounter upon being born into it, our parents were young. They most likely hadn't got their own personal lives figured out nor their relationship based on anything resembling the Principles of an Empowered Life. There was lots of inconsistency and unpredictability in our early experience of life.

2. In our very early experiences of life, focused as they were on the single undifferentiated being of *self*, we formed a basic and fundamental conclusion about the world and ourselves in it. This is not a reasoned and logical conclusion, but rather an *experiential* conclusion, in the Affective Mind. For most of us that conclusion is simple: "I get it! There is something wrong with me!" Now the world "makes sense!" That "there is something wrong with me" completely explains our experience. Most of us born into this "normal" world based our Belief System, our Fundamental Paradigm (our fundamental perception of Reality and ourselves in Reality) on this core conclusion: "*I'M NOT OK.*"

3. As our brain continued to develop, with the onset of language as a symbolic way of describing reality and our experience in it, cognition came—and with cognition, our ability to think, reason, and make decisions. Now our interaction with our

world shifted to a developing Cognitive Consciousness and the fundamental Affective conclusion about our fundamental flawedness <u>dropped out of sight</u> into the subconscious. That conclusion became the fundamental *Assumption* upon which our Reality was founded. It became, and remains, the primary filter through which we perceive Reality! Based on this *Assumption* and viewed through it *As A Filter*, our results and life experiences are ongoing and continuing evidences that <u>We Are Right</u> about not being OK<u>!</u>

4. As we continued to grow and develop in the "normal" world, we worked out strategies for survival based upon this fundamental conclusion that "there is something wrong with me; I'm not OK." In order to get some self-esteem and love out of life experiences that continually affirm that "I'm not capable," "I'm not lovable," "I'm not worthy," "I'm a victim and have little power or control in my own life," we developed manipulative strategies. This process continued vigorously from infancy through early grades. As we jockeyed to find our position in the world, in our family, in school, on the playground, among our friends, we developed manipulative strategies, strongly reinforced by our experience, that include such things as:
    a. Seeking acceptance and approval
    b. Controlling
    c. Hiding
    d. Bullying
    e. Maintaining an image of pretty, popular, smart, intelligent
    f. Emoting: crying, pouting, whining, throwing tantrums
    g. Personal appearance, body stuff
    h. Sex

5. These are strategies for gaining an experience of self-esteem and love. Employing such strategies yields an experience of life that is a *substitute* for <u>genuine self-esteem and self-love</u>, which would be based on the fundamental premise that "*I Am OK*; there is nothing wrong with me!" If the strategies work

and we get the "feels good" results we seek, they become *habits of living!* Note here that the "feels good" result of these strategies *is a fix!* Also note that the fix is a *substitute* for real self-esteem and love.

6. As we began to form relationships (starting very early in the family), we were drawn to those people with whom our strategies worked. The ongoing experience of "my strategies work" in relationship reinforces them as viable means to draw some self-esteem and love out of life experiences *and* simple strategies evolve from behaviors of habitual choice *to Addictions!* We habitually used these addictive behaviors to get our fixes!

7. An Addiction is a compulsive behavior that yields some sort of payoff, *a fix*. An Addiction is based on a physical *or psychological* "need" that is filled by resorting to a compulsive and habitual behavior for the *fix*. The "need" for self-esteem is met by a strategically employed compulsive behavior that provides the *fix*. The strategy and its fix have become an Addictive habit!

8. Following the pattern of relationship outlined in #6 above, Codependence results from the tendency of people with mutually compatible *Addictions* to find each other and form strategic relationships in which each gets his/her *fix*. For example, a man who fills his "need" for power (*his substitute* for love and self-esteem) by controlling behavior might hook up with a woman who fills her "need" for attention (*her substitute* for love and self-esteem) through being controlled. The participants *perceive subconsciously* that the other is filling their "need" for love and they *believe* and *perceive* that their relationship is based on love. They are "codependent" on each other for their respective *fixes!* "I *perceive* that she loves me because she obeys me." "I *perceive* that he loves me because even when he hurts me, he pays attention to me." It may be miserable, but *it works, codependently!* They are co-dependent on each other for their respective fixes.

9. Such a relationship works because the frames of reference of the participants are compatible, even though the relationship may be painful, dysfunctional, and demeaning.

10. People in codependency often escape from one such painful or demeaning relationship only to get into another of a similar nature *because* the internal Paradigm, the basic assumptions and conclusions about Reality, remain the same, and the subconsciously perceived needs and habitual strategies continue unaddressed! The Addictive Fix is still sought. Codependent patterns are in place. *Notice the patterns!* Codependence is a habit. It is an Addiction. *Codependency will be seen in the patterns!*

11. It should be noted that codependency results from conclusions drawn and strategies developed *in the past*, by a child. People in codependency are living as children in grown-up bodies. Playing childhood strategies in their relationships.

12. The solution for codependency lies in changing the fundamental paradigm. It lies in letting the child *Grow Up*. As adults, we do have a developed Cognitive mind. While the feelings and habits of the child (reinforced and "proven right" by many years of living) may scream loudly, we do have available an Adult Cognitive mind that can look, evaluate, consider, and make present-time choices. Adult cognitive decisions in the present may fly in the face of habits of behaving and feeling that have persisted since childhood. That inner child may not *Feel* like doing something different. In fact, quite strong feelings may arise! We may have to consciously <u>Put</u> *The Adult In Charge* and <u>make decisions</u> that *don't feel right* or *don't feel good*. However, Adult choices are consistent with adult perceptions and with available evidence in the present moment! "I don't *feel* capable of doing this, but I realize that as a grown-up man or woman, *I Can Do It!*" And on and on through the spectrum of challenges and opportunities we face as Adults.

13. The **first key** to overcoming codependency, then, is a willingness *To Be Wrong* about the beliefs we concluded as a child! And a willingness to *Risk* decisions and actions in order

to *explore* the world of the Adult that we have (at least in years) become. "Maybe I have been wrong all my life about my inability to have my life be any different than it has been!" "Maybe I really am a capable, lovable, worthy, empowerable human being!" "Maybe I do deserve to have genuine love and respect in my life!" "Maybe I really am capable of creating a satisfying life for myself!" "Maybe I really can participate in relationships that are rich and fulfilling!"

14. The **second key** to overcoming codependency is to *actually Accept Responsibility* for my entire life, including those conclusions that *I drew about Reality and myself in it* as an infant and child. If I drew those conclusions back then based on the experience of an infant and small child that have run my life for these many years, *and* those conclusions are not consistent with present-time adult perceptions and evidence, I can draw *different conclusions* today, based on the experience and perceptions of the adult that I am! Through consistent cognitive choice, I can reinforce my new conclusions and build <u>new habits of choosing</u> that are consistent with my present experience and perception. I can replace the childhood paradigm with an adult paradigm of Empowerment and growth.

15. *It's Never Too Late To Have A Happy Adulthood!*

The Empowered Life steps out of codependency. It accepts responsibility *for its own fulfillment.* The Empowered Relationship fosters physical, mental, and emotional health for You, Me, and Us, and shuns behaviors and attitudes that look like codependence.

Perhaps it might be useful for you to list below any patterns you can see in your own life that might give you clues to codependent tendencies you have. Patterns in relationships. Patterns in circumstances and situations. Patterns in your reactions to circumstances and situations. This is the time for real introspection. When you see the patterns, you have **Bear's** invitation to look-within where lays the *Only* real place for healing and transformation. There is lots of space! Most of us have lots of codependent tendencies.

-Notes to Self-

Chapter Eighteen—

Healing Codependence

Let's continue to consider codependence with emphasis on healing it and changing one's life. Codependency results from allowing the viewpoint, conclusions, habits and strategies of the child of long ago to determine our choices, feelings, and results today. Healing codependency is bringing our perceptions into the present and putting the adult in charge. It is allowing the adult with adult cognitive ability to *override* the feelings and habitual responses of the child within. I refer to "A Beautiful Mind" and John Nash again. Even with his schizophrenic delusions constantly present, *he chose* (in his adult cognitive mind) *to ignore them*. He chose to perceive his world *not* as it habitually appeared in his *perceived reality*, but in a manner consistent with a new reality *that worked for him in present time*. He *chose a new reality* and dedicated his mind and life energy to living in it! The portrayal in the movie of his success as a Nobel Laureate and the acknowledgement of him as a person (John Nash is a real person!) is testament to the capacity of the human spirit to accomplish this.

Here is the process, in nine steps.

First *Notice The Patterns*. The next few sentences contain the key to healing from codependency. Pay attention! [When you *get* these ideas (as deep realizations) and you put *responsibility* and *commitment* behind your getting of them, you are on your way to a new life!]

<u>Throughout all your relationships, life experiences, and life results, *You* are the one and only *Common Factor*. People and circumstances come and go in your life. *You* are the *one common element* that experiences, perceives, reacts, responds, chooses, decides, and takes action in all your relationships and in every moment of your life.</u> When you look at your life through that lens, the lens of you being the one common factor throughout your life, you will see the patterns. *It is never about circumstances or other people! It is always about you!* These patterns result from the fact that the conclusions you made as a child about reality and about you within it (comprising your box or

Paradigm) have determined your choices, your results, and how you have experienced *Everything* in your life since childhood. You will see patterns in your choices and your relationships and your sell-outs. Look until you find them and can acknowledge them! Keep a journal. Write down what you find, for they represent the beliefs that attract experience and cause patterns.

Second *Accept Responsibility*. *You* set up the **beliefs, conclusions, expectations, and strategies** that became your habits of perceiving, relating, and experiencing. You are not now nor ever have been a victim of anything. *You just decided and believed you were.* Life is. Unpleasant things happen. But *you,* always, from the beginning, every time, decided how you would interpret them, respond to them, and fit them into your reality.

Third *Accept That You May Have Been Wrong*. When you see the patterns *and* your futile attempts to escape from repeating unpleasant experiences, *and* you accept that you are the only common element through all of it, you might wonder if perhaps your perceptions of yourself and your reality might be the real root of it all. Maybe your perceptions, based on your beliefs and expectations, which drove your reactions in the past, are not working very well in present time. Let's be so bold as to say they are not relevant now. Perhaps if you changed your perceptions of yourself and your reality, you might break out of the patterns!

Fourth **Look At Your Present World Through The Mind And Cognitive Ability Of The Adult**. You are no longer a child. You have a wonderful thinking, well-developed, reasoning adult brain. You can look out at events, people, and circumstances and conclude what makes sense in the present. Your adult brain can reason, from present-time observations, what makes sense *Now*. Are you really as incapable as you feel? Are you really as unlovable as you feel? Do you really deserve what you are experiencing? Are you really locked into these patterns? Can you really change your life? What do you want? What if you gave it a shot now and put your energy behind creating what you want? Could you, as an adult, actually accomplish it?

Fifth **Define The Reality You Want To Experience**. Look at yourself through adult perceptions. Note your strengths, your abilities, your talents, your interests, your dreams, your visions for the future, your desired relationships. Based on the sum total of life's experience, who are you (in a Being sense; remember Be-Do-Have?)? How would your life be if it truly expressed and manifested the abilities and attributes you possess and that are important to you? Start writing these things down. Write a description of the life that would magnify and honor who you really are. If you want some additional support in this, go to true friends who will tell you the truth (review Chapter 13 on Feedback). Give yourself some time and space for this. You are literally describing and defining a new Reality for yourself!

Sixth *Separate Your Choices-To-Action From Your Feelings*. Your feelings in a given set of circumstances are your habitual reactions based on the conclusions of the child. Way back then, the world looked the way it looked to that child. Back then, you assigned meanings and interpretations to perceptions within a belief set formulated by the child with the resources of a child. The world may have been scary, intimidating, overpowering, and painful. In that world the child may have seen itself as ugly, fat, lonely, unworthy, dirty, used, and a victim. To that child, a set of strategies were developed that made sense in dealing with such a perceived world. Within the paradigm of those strategies, feelings were consistent with perceptions. *The feelings became automatic, habitual responses to habitual perceptions, the vestiges of the child.* But *Now* they are just vestiges! Circumstances may trigger vestigial feelings. And present circumstances may trigger *old feelings* that are tied into past circumstances, *not necessarily* present circumstances.

Stop, look, and think. Your cognitive mind can pause, bring you into the present, and evaluate whether your feelings are *really* consistent with *present* reality. Even in the illness of his schizophrenia, John Nash learned to *ignore* feelings and perceptions that were inconsistent with what his adult cognitive mind *knew* was present reality. You can learn to separate your habitual vestigial feelings from what you *know* you perceive in present time. It may not *feel* right. It may *feel* scary or embarrassing. But you can *know* it *is* possible, and *is* right for your growth and progress. And you can base your choices-to-act on what you *know* to be consistent with present reality.

Seventh *Be Willing To Risk New Choices In Your Present-Time World.* You will come to experience a new kind of feeling as an indicator of good choices. It is a *feeling of satisfaction* that comes when you are true to yourself in present time. While you are feeling all those crazy feelings of the child screaming through its perceptions and beliefs (they may not ever completely go away!), you will come to recognize a calm, inner sense of **satisfaction**, the inner knowing that your present choices are consistent with what you want. At first, you will *feel* those past feelings with a vengeance. Your inner child will be screaming in fear and discomfort. Now you put the adult in charge. Your adult self, in present time, can take care of the child. He or she did not have such an adult to assist in forming a more workable perception of the world back then, but you can provide one now! The world that did not make sense back then, can make sense now. The *adult you* can allow that child to grow up! You can provide the safety, the protection, and the shield. You can create the reality *now* that the child did not perceive back then. You can provide an experience of Trust of Self NOW that the child did not have back then. And you can take the risks now to test out and refine that reality that the child never dared to take! Remember, risk is just that! Things may not work just right the first time you try something, or even several times as you try it. That things don't immediately work out is *not* evidence that the child was right! Keep risking! Keep the adult mind in charge! Base your life on the Principles of Growth and Empowerment! The Adult Cognitive you, with that marvelous adult human brain capable of thinking, reasoning, evaluating, concluding anew, will eventually find what does work and your life will change in the process.

Eighth, **Surround Yourself With A Support Group**. This is critical! Find people who are *true friends*. Look among those who assisted you in writing your new definition of your Reality. True friends are **not enablers**. They absolutely *WILL NOT* buy your victim stories, pander to your feelings and fears, sympathize with your whines and cries, and enable your dysfunctional behaviors. They will support your commitment to heal. They probably *already see the magnificent you* that you have hidden from yourself beneath your childhood filters. They don't live in your box, so they see you from outside of it! To recognize such people, review the Fundamental Issues of Support and Applying the Principles of Growth in Section One of this book. Share with your support circle the new Definition of Reality you have written. Enroll them in being true supporters of your process. Share with them the Fundamental Issues of Support and that you truly want them to support you from those decisions. Being with such people may not at first *feel comfortable*, because they are holding you to your commitment. Being with such people may at first produce in you anger, frustration, negative reaction, etc. Remember, these are the feelings of that child throwing a tantrum. He or she has been in charge a long time and may not relinquish control willingly. That child has only found "safety" in its world by containing that world within a childish set of beliefs, expectations and strategies. You must allow that child to find out that your adult world is OK and safe and that you can handle it just fine. Good friends who support you in that endeavor are priceless!

Ninth **Persist, Don't Give Up!** You will be faced with all those habitual feelings from the past. If you want to heal, you need to stay the course. Keep in mind the price you are willing to pay to heal. WIT! Keep going. Keep your true friends around you. Be willing to feel your feelings. Keep your conscious mind in charge of your decisions. Make decisions that are consistent with adult perceptions in present time. Keep risking. Hang in there! Call on **Elk** and the spirit of stamina. You will break out of codependency into a whole new world of Empowerment and Self-Esteem.

Perhaps it might be useful for you to write down below how you will implement the nine steps to heal codependency in your life. Visualize and put down in writing what your life looks like as you implement each step. Identify and list candidates for your personal support group. These are friends and loved ones who are so committed and so caring that they will not enable you and will hold you to your implementation! When you get yourself and your support group enrolled in your healing process, you will succeed!

-Notes to Self-

Chapter Nineteen—

Dealing with Serious Differences

With regard to the statement in the Chapter 16 that bagging the relationship is a last resort for Empowered Individuals, what about when the differences are serious? We may be hanging out in hope that something will change on its own, or waiting in fear of dire consequences if we bring up a serious or sensitive subject for discussion.

With regard to "hope," one takes either of two positions in life: Ownership or Victimhood. *Waiting* in "hope" is Victimhood. Ownership is proactive, accepting and taking responsibility for one's life. There is no "truth" out there. Only one's perception of truth. (If you are still struggling with this idea, go back and ponder Chapters 1 and 14.) You have your perceptions and they make up your truth. Everyone else has their individual perceptions and they make up their individual truths. The reality of life is that *no two people on the planet have exactly the same perception of truth all the time*. One makes a decision on what "truth" is for oneself, at the moment of decision, and then makes subsequent decisions accordingly.

Every decision or choice has consequences. *The thing that keeps one "waiting in hope" with regard to serious differences is the fear of consequences from bringing it up.* Life is Risk and the only "hope" is that the consequences of one's choices bring about learning early enough so that both perceptions and choices can be refined and a reasonably satisfying life experience forged. The majority of people on the planet (probably the *vast* majority) don't get this and they actually believe their perception of truth *Is True* and is fixed. So we engage in right/wrong struggles with each other instead of accepting that both of us (all of us) *Are Right* (all the time) because we see the reality we see and none of us sees exactly the same reality as anyone else. We refuse to believe that our perceptions are flexible! The troubles of the world are caused among people who are inflexible in their perceptions of what it true!

We are *all* right, in our perceptions. The problem, therefore, is not Who is Right? Rather, it is how do we make decisions together when joint decisions must be made and we see things differently? In families, marriages, and relationships, this is the critical issue. Even among nations! Most people don't work out the mechanisms for making joint decisions when they see things differently, so fighting, conflicts, and divorces result from their choices to avoid or ignore this simple principle.

Sometimes there are differences involving violations of beliefs or expectations that are so painful or disruptive that it is evident that serious differences exist in the *basic definition* of the relationship.

With regard to serious differences in your relationship, there are exactly four options. That's right, exactly four! Pick one. In the spirit of What-Do-I-Want? and WIT, pick one!

Option One: Accept the circumstances that you have in your relationship as though they will never change and *genuinely and forever* come to peace with them, *because the benefits you experience in the relationship are more important to you than the frustrations.* This is coming to grips *with your priorities* in such a way that you truly come to inner peace with things (inside of you!) and forever stop whining, complaining, feeling bad, and further discussion of the subject. Find inner peace through real introspective clarity of priorities. Find it through acceptance of irritations of lower priority in favor of blessings of higher priority. This requires clearly identifying *small stuff* issues as just that, *small stuff.* Realize that it is up to you to deal with the *small stuff.* It is certainly all right to discuss them, then accept the outcome of the discussion and let them go, forever! The beauty of Option One is that your *perception* of the differences *has shifted* through inner clarity of priorities, and inner peace comes in the shift! (Remember Viktor Frankl?)

Option Two: Take proactive steps through honest, forthright, and open communication with your partner to change the circumstances. This comes from accepting yourself as OK in your perceptions of truth, others as OK in theirs (especially your partner!), making the assumption that everyone wants things to be good for all, ***and*** *initiating action* to bring that about–**Win/Win**. This is a choice requiring courage and commitment! Serious and sincere communications take place between the two (or all) of you. After the conversations and communications of Option Two are held and taken to as much completion as seems to be possible, you have two remaining choices: accept *any* results and changes *As **Gifts** from the other* to be received with joy and gratitude, without any further expectations, and go to Option One, *Or* failing that, go to Option Three. Option One may not work when you truly cannot accept the results. In the real world, there are genuine differences between people's perceptions and values that cannot be resolved. Option Three IS a real and viable option!

Option Three: If Option One does not provide inner peace and satisfaction, and/or Option Two does not produce acceptable and satisfactory results, take proactive steps to get out of the circumstances. This is another choice requiring courage and commitment! This is choosing *Not To Play* anymore. If Options One and Two do not produce inner peace and satisfaction, *this may be the kindest and most loving step you can take!* In the world of the Empowered, terminating the relationship is a real and ultimate possibility. It requires and deserves honest acceptance of the outcome without judgment.

Option Four: Do nothing. Sell out to fear of consequences and avoidance, and settle for a life of recurring frustration, whining, complaining, resentment, victimhood, and a growing cancer that will silently eat at your own self-esteem and the remaining fabric of the relationship until it is barren and devoid of joy. In this, you will be joining the majority of people on the planet in their mutual sympathy-seeking, whiny, story-telling, gossipy lives as victims, complaining and blaming (life's a bitch and then we die!).

That's it. Those are the four. Pick one.

"Option Five" (careful, this is only temporary!): There might be a fifth and temporary option that *could* be legitimately selected <u>for a while</u> (but *be careful! It is tempting to hang out here, making it into Option Four, and avoid the Real Truth!*). Wait around and gather more data. This option is a form of "hope" based on the belief that what one has experienced and perceived is somehow incomplete or inaccurate, that the patterns one has observed and experienced are not really what is going on *in totality* and maybe a bigger picture will eventually emerge if one waits and observes long enough. Be careful! This could be legitimate, but hanging out here could actually be avoidance of consequences! Hang here long enough and you might transform the situation into Option Four and get stuck with "what you have!" Many people hang out here in justification for a lifetime, only to eventually die in misery! ***Consider this: people who operate in this "Option" may be living in order to die; they never really live because of fear of what might happen at death.***

[By the way, *as an exercise in personal empowerment,* try pondering these four, maybe five, options in connection with your own relationship *with yourself!* This is a real **Bear** exercise!]

If one could find a partner who shared in significant ways a commitment to Options One and Two, one would have a wonderful opportunity to create a truly Empowered Partnership filled with Joy and Growth for each and both! In such an Empowered Partnership, even serious differences have a chance of being resolved in satisfying ways. Remember, for two people to be together, they don't have to agree on what's right. They just have to want to be together. If that sounds simple, try it sometime!

Let's go back to the four options I outlined and explore numbers two and four more fully. The only way I know to really change the world around us in a real and empowering way is Option Two. It requires two things of either or both (or all): 1) The people involved really want something better and at least one or more is (are) willing to take a risk to initiate open and honest communication on the subject, and/or 2) the one desiring the change gets very clear on personal priorities and makes a decision. He or she then takes a stand ("This is critically important to me. I want the change bad enough to risk a lot, *even the relationship if necessary!*"). The objective of initiating Option Two in this manner is to get the attention of the other(s) to the *importance* of the subject, and if it is *a relationship-risking subject,* to help the other see the ***critical*** *importance* of the subject! "This is *really* troubling me and unless we address it, our relationship is in jeopardy!" This is the attention-getting spirit of **Owl**! It is being truly honest with self!

The world operates on WIIFM (What's In It For Me?). In relationship stuff this means just because one person is bothered, that is not necessarily the other person's problem. It becomes important to the other person when something *vital to the other person* is jeopardized; the other senses a loss of something they value, i.e., relationship, stability, income, sex, eating, companionship. In the "ideal" relationship, the feelings of each partner are important to the other and feelings of hurt are an unacceptable consequence. In many relationships, this is not the case and one partner may be insensitive to the needs and feelings of the other. Failure to recognize *or care* that I am bothering you suggests that your feelings are less important to me than some personal ego stuff (e.g., Being Right or getting my way).

In ordinary disempowered relationships, such failures and their consequences are truly less important than one's own self-centered view. However, if the "offending" partner perceives great enough consequences, then WIIFM sets in. That person is motivated to engage in the Option Two discussion to protect *His/Her* interest in the issue. You find out what WIIFM is for your partner and *engage on that level*, and something *will* happen. You will get attention to the issue. Is this manipulation? Not if it is *not attached to outcomes*. It is not intended to manipulate or change the partner, rather it is a sincere cry for attention to something that in the reality of the one initiating, is critically important to the health, perhaps the continuance of the relationship. Its only desired outcome is honest and open communication on the issue.

You can keep on waiting for more data or more courage, but the only way to get change is to take action, *proactively!* And that means taking a risk! If only life could have been set up so that we could just be victims, wait for the lottery, and live happily ever after. Unfortunately (*or fortunately* to one seeking Empowerment!), for most of us life is risk and the first three options outlined *are the only way* to ultimate satisfaction and joy.

The child feels. The adult thinks. Putting the adult in charge means making your decision based on smart adult thinking in present time. Stop, look, and think. Stop the old patterns. Look at what is actually going on in your circumstances, look at the options you have, look at the consequences of choosing each of the various options. Think about those options and weigh and evaluate all of them. Go ahead and feel your feelings, nothing wrong with feelings, and then take a risk and *do* the *smart* thing!

There is a lot of meat in this chapter. If your mind is not a-buzz with introspective contemplation and opportunities, you might want to spend time re-reading and pondering! Further, you might find it useful to list below some issues and frustrations in your primary relationships and how you can apply Options One and Two. Life is too short to spend it in anger, resentment, and frustration! "Man is that he might have joy."

-Notes to Self-

Chapter Twenty—

Advanced Principles of Relationship

This is a summary in outline form of what I term Advanced Principles of Relationship. That title embodies my experience that only a few relationships actually get to a point where they are truly based on these principles, consequently these are "advanced" principles. This is a summary then of the fundamental principles of *a truly Empowered Relationship*.

Advanced Principles of Relationship

1. I accept total responsibility for my own experience ("I know my being triggered has nothing to do with you!").
2. I realize that I cannot ever fully comprehend *your* perception of reality and therefore I have no business judging it.
3. I realize that both you and I are totally magnificent Human Beings, that both you and I are in the process of discovering and expressing our magnificence, that you and I both want joy and happiness in life and relationship, and that each of us is struggling in our own personal ways to find it. I want to support you in your struggle, and want you to support me in mine.
4. I accept responsibility for satisfying my own self-esteem needs. You owe me nothing. When I want something from you, I will be responsible for asking for what I want, instead of expecting you to give it to me spontaneously. I will take nothing for granted and be grateful for what you do give me, accepting it as a gift.
5. I commit to learning and using together a tool like the "Conflict Dialogue" to reduce or eliminate conflict in our relationship.
6. When I am living true to who I am, I realize that your being triggered results from stuff in your past and that when triggered, you are not likely to be in present time, but are somewhere in the past emotionally and spiritually. When you are triggered, I know

you are experiencing me as filling a role in your Paradigm that was once filled by someone else, a parent, sibling, friend, teacher, etc., and that your expectations around that role are rooted in the past. Therefore, instead of *reacting* to you in such a moment, I will honor your space, or ask you for what you want or need and be available; that includes giving you the space you need to resolve the issue by yourself.

7. I assume that we each want the best for ourselves and each other in life and in our relationship at all times, especially when we don't agree on what is right.

8. I recognize that personal neediness comes from conclusions we each made as small children and that these needy conclusions lead to codependence. I will strive to become healthy enough as an adult that I can supply my own self-esteem resources and don't depend on you to meet them. We are together *not* because we need each other, but rather because we simply want to be together.

9. I recognize in general that I can either *Be Right* or have relationship. I generally can't have both!

Perhaps you might find it useful to take an introspective inventory of your relationship, especially your primary relationship, with respect to these Advanced Principles. Write down your observations and any opportunities you see for improvement and self-development.

-Notes to Self-

Section Five—
The Empowered Life

Chapter Twenty One—

Play to Win vs. Play Not to Lose

Back to counting things again. This time it's playing the game of life. There are two ways to play the game of life:

Play to Win
or
Play Not to Lose

Play to Win means playing at the edge, taking risks, giving it all. Play to Win means pressing limits, pushing to expand one's life, seeking growth and self-discovery. It means stepping far outside of comfort zone, playing near the edge of one's life, perhaps even stepping over that edge. The person playing to win *knows* that losing is possible, perhaps has experienced it more than once, and accepts that possibility. The person playing to win accepts that mistakes are likely, even unavoidable, and are never grounds for condemnation but are actually opportunities to grow and improve.

The person playing to win is motivated primarily by vision, opportunity and possibility. The person playing to win focuses on Being and results and *seeks* feedback from both results and from other players, surrounding oneself with true friends who communicate openly and honestly. Mind chatter sounds like: What can I learn from this? Who has useful feedback for me? How can I improve? What is a better way to do this?

Playing to win is accompanied by *extremes of feelings*, ranging from fear and disappointment to excitement and exhilaration. The person playing to win accepts these extremes of feelings and doesn't shrink from them or avoid them, even thrives on them. The person playing to win knows that such extremes of feelings go along with the territory of winning.

Play Not to Lose means playing where it is safe, well within comfort zone, avoiding risks, playing only hard enough to stay in the game. Playing not to lose means focusing on saving face, looking at least acceptable, worrying that losing is possible and fearing that possibility, being motivated primarily by need for approval, fear of loss (loss of approval, loss of security, loss of possessions, etc.), salvaging image, hiding actual results. The person playing not to lose tells lots of stories and gives excuses for mediocre results, and even comes to believe the stories as justifications for mediocre behavior and activity.

For the person playing not to lose, stories revolve around activities performed. Energy is spent in doing activities rather than in accomplishing results. The person playing not to lose wants to *be seen* doing the activities. Doing the activities is justification for expending the energy. Do-Have-Be. Mind chatter sounds like: Well, at least I tried, *at least I. . . .*Such a person is focused in the past, looking for past accomplishments as evidence of self-worth in the face of beliefs of not-OK that are supported by mediocre results in the present. Playing not to lose is an attempt to avoid extremes of feelings.

I suppose there could be noted a third way to play the game of life, namely to quit. This is expressed in such things as suicide and insanity. For the rest of us, the game goes on, playing to win, or playing not to lose.

The Empowered Life is Playing to Win. No question about it. This person has nothing to hide because he or she has accepted self as OK. *Being OK is associated with <u>existing</u> and is independent of results.* It is Be-Do-Have. There is nothing to prove. The person playing to win accepts that losing is a real possibility and will likely occur from time to time. Risking, exploring, and growth are the Stuff of Life! Learning and improvement always result from choices made and consequences observed. Feedback is welcome. Life is lived forward, into vision, moving toward achievement of what might be possible, focusing on What-Do-I-Want. Risk is accepted, even welcomed. Comfort and safety are only temporary resting places, with the realization that there is no growth there. Life is exciting and exhilarating, sometimes challenging, and always worthwhile. There is always something new to learn and experience.

How are you playing?

It might be useful for you to list below evidences you can see in your life of how you are playing. Feedback from your friends and primary relationships will support self-honesty here! Denial is an awful trap along the path to Empowerment!

-Notes to Self-

Chapter Twenty Two—

Strive For vs. Settle For

With respect to any quality or characteristic of being human, there is variation. Take height for example. Human beings range in height from the shortest among us to the tallest. If we looked at all the heights in any group, counting the number of people in each category, and plotted these numbers on a graph, it would look something like this figure. The horizontal axis is the varying height from smallest to tallest. The vertical axis is the number of people in each category.

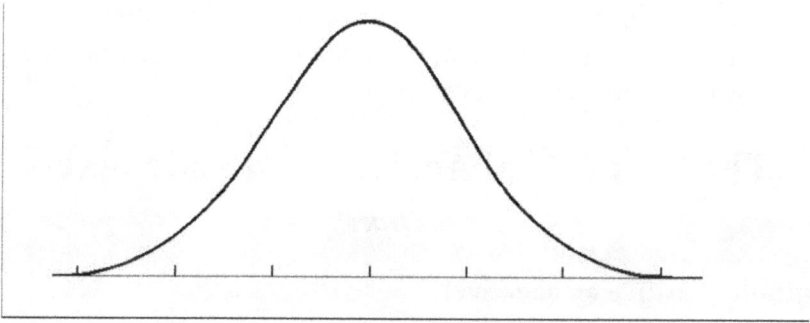

This is called the Normal Distribution or Bell-shaped Curve. It describes the distribution of virtually any characteristic, physical and mental, in a large population. Looking at height, for example, the Normal Distribution shows that in any large population of people, at the shortest height end of the scale there is one person, the shortest person in the population. As height increases, the number of people in each height category increases. Most people are in the middle range of the diagram, with the peak of the diagram occurring at the average height of people. The number diminishes again in the taller range to that one person who is the tallest one in the population.

The Normal Distribution can be used to describe the distribution of just about any human characteristic, such as, for example, athletic ability, from the least able to the amazing champions. It can describe ability to sing from the least able to the greatest concert soloist or the ability to build cabinets from the least competent to the greatest. It describes every human characteristic. In all these characteristics, and in every human characteristic, most people fall in the middle range with diminishing numbers in both tails of the curve.

And now take you. With respect to every possible human ability and characteristic, you fall on the respective curves somewhere. You are in the middle range regarding most characteristics, and you fall on the low tail with respect to some and you fall on the upper scale with respect to some others. The point is that no one is remarkable in all possible human characteristics and no one is lacking in all possible human characteristics. All human beings have areas of strength where they easily succeed and areas of weakness where they struggle to grow and learn. It is in these areas of growth and learning where effort and energy must be expended. Below is a chart that presents, in order, the Elements of Success in any area of life.

The Elements of Achievement and Success

In Order!

Attitude (positive or negative)

> *How do you feel about your life and circumstances? The Universe doesn't care whether you like life and the things you face in life! Your employer, your boss, your customer, your teacher, none of these particularly care whether you like your circumstances or not. They just expect results. You are the one who has to care. You decide your attitude about the circumstances of your life.*

Belief (in self and the value of your effort)

> *Do you believe that you can succeed or achieve? Do you believe in the worth of your cause? The Universe doesn't care whether you believe you can succeed or not! Your employer, your boss, your customer, your teacher, none of these particularly care whether you believe you can succeed or not, or whether you believe in the worth of your efforts. They just expect results. You are the one who has to believe. You decide to believe in yourself.*

Priorities (how you spend your time and effort)

You have the same 24 hours, 7 days, 12 months as every other human being. How you use your time and life energy is completely up to you. You have the same amount of time as every successful person, and as every failure! You have exactly the same 24/7/365 as the leaders of business, government, education and every human endeavor. You make the decisions on using your time. You can use it to play around, mope around, or to learn, grow, and accomplish— and don't forget balance; play matters, also.

Ability—*Ability falls far below the other three! Your ability is the least important quality to succeed, and it falls in two areas.*

> **Innate Ability.** *This comes with the package of you. It derives primarily from the genetic package that makes you up and your fundamental Being.*

> **Educatable Ability.** *You have total control over this. It increases with training, schooling, experience, and effort. If you need to learn something in order to succeed, go for it!*

Consider the Elements of Success chart. These elements are presented *In Order*. Note that the lowest Element of Success and Achievement is Ability. Your ability is *not* the primary determinant of your success!

The first and most important is Attitude. Your attitude about yourself, your life, your opportunities, your challenges, your circumstances, is completely up to you. You choose your attitude. Nothing in the Universe demands any particular attitude. In the common mind, certain attitudes may be commonly associated with certain circumstances. Negative attitudes may be commonly associated with negative experiences. But nothing about the circumstance or experience *Demands* any particular attitude. Remember Viktor Frankl? He survived Auschwitz. He found himself surrounded with unspeakably horrible circumstances, but he discovered he could choose his attitude! If you choose to have a negative attitude about anything, it diminishes your likelihood of success. It is your choice. Empowerment requires that you accept responsibility for your attitude.

The second element is **Belief**. Whether you believe you can, or whether you believe you can't, *you're right!* And you are the one who set up your beliefs and your Belief System. ***Your past results are not necessarily evidence of your ability. They are primarily evidence of your attitude, belief and priorities, back then.*** Having focused your attention on *Now* and having identified what you want in your future, you can now decide to believe in your capacity to achieve it! Empowered individuals realize that their Belief System is flexible and they can alter it to create the results they want. You decide whether you believe you can. . . !

The third element is your **Priorities**. You have the same 24/7/365 as every other person on the planet. Think about your hero, that person who most exemplifies or models what you want in your life. That person has a positive attitude and positive beliefs about achieving, and has, *and uses* the same 24/7/365 effectively to make it real. There are innumerable examples of people of average "ability" who, with the same 24/7/365 as you have, put forth whatever effort it takes to achieve remarkable results. Those are the examples who demonstrate the underlying truth of the message of this book. Decide to emulate them and join them!

Finally, and lowest on the chart, is **Ability**. You see, ability is *not* the determining factor in success! If what you want requires acquiring education or training, then use your 24/7/365 to acquire whatever you need. Note that **Educatable Ability** is totally under your control and up to your choice. If you need to learn something to achieve what you want, go do it!

Let's go back to the Normal Distribution diagram at the beginning of this chapter. It says that you are somewhere on the respective bell shaped curve with respect to everything about you. If you are on the lower tail regarding something that is relevant to what you want, that simply means that you may have to *arrange your priorities* to augment it, to develop it, to train it, to learn it, to acquire it, to express it. You may have to spend more time developing that quality or acquiring that resource than someone who falls higher on the curve with respect to it. Does that discourage you? Remember, *you choose your attitude*. And remember WIT! Fast learner or slow learner, anyone can master a subject!

Which brings us to the title of this chapter, *Strive For vs. Settle For*. Here is that mirror again. Look in the mirror of your life, your results, your attitude. Do you *strive for things*, proactively? Or do you settle for things, simply accepting life as it comes and resigning yourself to circumstances. In school, do you (did you) settle for Cs and Bs? Or do you (did you) strive for As, because it was never OK for you to settle for less? What is (was) your attitude about your grades? How about other areas of your life? Do you strive for higher results and achievements or are you willing to settle for what happens to come your way? The effort you are willing to expend is an exact manifestation of your priorities! Do you strive to grow and learn in order to achieve visionary goals, or do you settle for what you have and what, in your resignation, you believe you are only capable of giving to the world? Your potential lies mostly in the area of unexplored life!

Regarding education, I am concerned about students who settle for Bs and Cs. Even a B represents only around 80% achievement in learning. Picture yourself on a gurney in the operating room with a crowd of folks in green scrubs surrounding you. In a moment you will go into the la-la land of anesthetic and those people will be digging around inside you. Just before you disappear into unconsciousness, the thought occurs to you, "Did they get solid As in the subjects that are important to me now? Could they have graduated from their training with Bs, or even Cs, in those subjects? Is the stuff that is vital to me fully mastered by them?"

In my wanderings through life, at one point I needed to get a certification as a Natural Gas Technician. It required taking a class and passing a test. I was in a room with several other candidates. I noticed the gentleman sitting next to me spent most of his time copying from my paper. When we took the test, he continued this behavior. I got my certificate with a high score, as I presume did he. He's out there somewhere, presenting himself as a Certified Gas Technician to employers and homeowners. If he were to come to your home and showed you his certificate, would you *expect* that he had mastery of the knowledge and consistent and demonstrable competence pertaining to installation of gas lines and appliances? How about *every* professional who provides a product or service to you? If you knew they cheated, or only achieved Bs and Cs in their training, would you be happy and satisfied with them performing their service for you? You owe to those who depend on you, or will ever depend on you, to deliver to them exactly what you expect from those you depend on! Mastery!

I strongly believe that whatever our field of learning and performance in life, we owe it to our children, our customers, our employers, our patients, to those who will depend on our performance, to *master* the subjects relevant to what we deliver to them. Whatever it takes!

No matter where you are on the Normal Distribution regarding any particular quality that is relevant to What You Want, you must decide whether you are willing to *strive for* improving it and MASTERING it, or whether you are willing to *settle for* mediocrity or leaving it the way it is. That is your decision to make. If you choose to Strive For, then you will always look for the resources that are available to you to climb higher on the path to accomplishment, to learn, to grow, to develop yourself and your means, to achieve your dreams! Solid A grades are the only acceptable outcomes for the Empowered!

Perhaps you might find it useful to take an honest look at your priorities. Remember, what you have in your life is an exact mirror of your priorities! Keep a log of exactly how you use your time for an entire week. Log every use of time, in terms of every minute. Then examine it critically with respect to how it supports what you say you want. This is a critical opportunity to Get Real! Write down below changes you are willing to make to bring your priorities in line with your goals.

-Notes to Self-

Chapter Twenty Three—

I'm OK, You're OK

There is a little branch of psychology called Transactional Analysis. To understand the transactions among people, transactional psychologists recognize that people come from three psychological positions in their interpersonal interactions (i.e., transactions): Parent, Child, and Adult. These positions can be considered to be *strategic interactive role states* that we adopt in response to roles that we assign to ourselves and others in our basic perception (paradigm) of the game of life. To understand *strategic interactive role states,* you might want to review Chapter 17 on Codependence and how people develop manipulative strategies to experience love. Here is a brief summary of the characteristics of these strategic role states.

Parent	*power, authoritarian, controlling, teaching, correcting, reacting, judging, generally a position of top-dog in the game of* ***"Right/Wrong"***
Child	*submissive, victim, playful, fighting, bullying, reacting, emotional, generally a position of bottom-dog with respect to Parent in the game of "**Right/Wrong**"*
Adult	*equal, impartial, neutral, observing, logical, non-judging, boundaried, responding, self-honest, learning, doesn't get involved in the game of "**Right/Wrong**"*

The following transactions illustrate transactions that work. They may not be pleasant or growth-producing or healing, and they may be actually destructive or demeaning, but they work, because they share a common or compatible frame of reference. They are *strategic interactive role states* employed by grown-ups playing life from the Belief-System-filtered perceptions of their inner child; adults who are utilizing the manipulative strategies of one (grown-up) child interacting with another (grown-up) child. They are based on the Belief System conclusions the child made about itself in its past world that was dominated by the parent. The transactions in column one are identified by the roles played. The viewpoint in column two is expressed as coming from the childhood self of the *first position* in column one, with respect to its assignment of role to the *second*. Many marriages are built upon one or more of these transactions!

Patriarchal and Matriarchal relationships are fundamentally of these transactional types. These transactions are common in the disempowered world and in disempowered relationships. They are dramatically present in codependent relationships. Most interactions among the disempowered and codependent people of the world are really just grown-up versions of the grade school playground. Perhaps you recognize them and have been involved in them yourself.

Transaction	*Viewpoint*
Parent-Child	*(I hope I'm OK, you're not OK; but the parent is OK and I hope to experience being OK by pretending to be the parent and dominating you to make you the person I want you to be)*
Child-Parent	*(I'm not OK, you're OK. See, I'm right!)*
Child-Child	*(I'm not OK, you're not OK; but the parent is OK and I hope to experience being OK by pretending to be the parent and dominating you, OR I get to be right about not being OK by letting you dominate me—it's a playground game!)*
Parent-Parent	*(I don't know if I'm OK and I don't know if you're OK; all I know is that the parent is OK, the child is not OK, and I'm trying to feel OK by pretending to be the parent)*

The only transaction involving *Adult* that works is:

ADULT-ADULT *(I'm OK, you're OK. We interact in present time as the adults we are. Neither of us has to pretend anything.)*

Adult does not share a common or compatible frame of reference with either of the other two positions and cannot sustain a transaction with them. One person or the other must withdraw or the transaction breaks down. The dance ends. For *true* Partnership to work, it must be based on *Adult-Adult* transactions. An Empowered Life participating in an Empowered Relationship is based fundamentally on Adult-Adult transactions. The Adult position is based on a deep acceptance of the fundamental premise of the Empowered Life that

I'm OK and You're OK.

As my own children have grown to adulthood, I have reflected seriously and often on how I did as a parent and father. As with many parents in many families, I made discoveries of Principles of Growth and Empowerment too late for my children to have experienced much from an "enlightened father" during their formative years. I did my best, but my best was immature. Wisdom and learning about life seem to come with age and experience.

In the traditional native village, the job of teaching the children was given to the grandfathers and grandmothers, the Elders. The parents were busy making the living, out doing the things that took care of the village and their families. To the community, the Elders have learned from life experiences and have gained wisdom. Thus, Wisdom was the foundation of teaching the youth.

We have it all screwed up in our so-called modern "civilized" culture. Education of our children is based on knowledge, not wisdom. We send the elders off to rest homes, the elders move to retirement communities, or the children move away

from their parents and take the grandchildren with them. We have separated our youth from their grandparents and from the wisdom of the generations. My several grandchildren all live hundreds of miles from me. If I have learned anything in my life about empowered and resourceful living, what opportunity do I have to share it with my grandchildren by direct experience together with regular opportunities for communication and sharing of wisdom?

Can you relate to this? In our age of "enlightenment," we have separated the youth from the generational anchors of wisdom and values. They float, disconnected from the principles that work, the anchors of their heritage, the enduring values, seeking to find them on their own in drugs, sex, and social experiment. We see the results in the instabilities of relationship and society!

Is it really possible for human parents to learn and *really* **Get** these principles early enough in their lives and in large enough numbers to raise a new generation of youth, a new generation who are empowered enough to create a new world, based on personal responsibility, inner-directness, and respect for others and community?

I have concluded that the fundamental job of parents *is* to raise what we might term *truly mature adults*. The world is full of children in grown-up bodies. It is not hard to raise *them*. Children in grown-up bodies raise more children in grown-up bodies! The challenge is to raise truly mature adults.

Truly mature adults are characterized by the four Rs.

Responsible
Respectful
Resilient
Resourceful

Such people are empowered, live empowered lives, deal with others respectfully, and learn and grow from the challenges of life. They live confidently, knowing they have the inner resources to deal with life's challenges and create satisfaction in their lives. Their relationships are empowered. They are the givers and contributors to the world. The world is made better because they live in it and their legacy lives on through their children and those they empower by example and encouragement. To contribute to a world full of such people, this book, my work, and the remainder of my life are dedicated. An arrogant statement? To me it is a vision of purpose and possibility.

Perhaps you might find it useful below to look in the mirror of your relationships and your transactions, and write down what you see. Where do you hang out in the Parent-Child-Adult spectrum? Then give some thought to what kind of world you want to live in and the world you want your posterity to live in. Write down the vision you have for that world and some thoughts on what you intend to commit to in order to bring it about.

-Notes to Self-

Chapter Twenty Four—

Closing the Circle

A little device was once shown to me called the Johari Window, first designed by Joseph Luft and Harry Ingham, [Joseph Luft, (1970, 2nd Ed.) *Group processes; an introduction to group dynamics.* Palo Alto, CA: National Press Books.]. The Johari Window is a two by two matrix with four cells. Across the top and down the sides are titles of concepts such that each cell represents the idea expressed in the combination of the two concepts. The variation of the Johari Window that I find useful here brings closure to the Medicine Circle with which we began this journey. Its titles across the top and down the side are: **I Don't Know** and **I Know.**

THE STAGES OF TRANSFORMATION

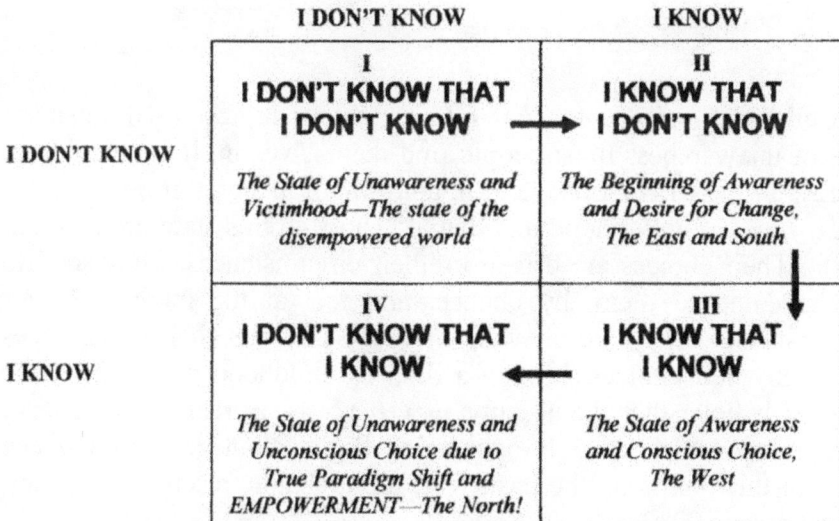

	I DON'T KNOW	I KNOW
I DON'T KNOW	**I** **I DON'T KNOW THAT** **I DON'T KNOW** → *The State of Unawareness and Victimhood—The state of the disempowered world*	**II** **I KNOW THAT** **I DON'T KNOW** *The Beginning of Awareness and Desire for Change, The East and South*
I KNOW	**IV** **I DON'T KNOW THAT** **I KNOW** ← *The State of Unawareness and Unconscious Choice due to True Paradigm Shift and EMPOWERMENT—The North!*	**III** **I KNOW THAT** **I KNOW** *The State of Awareness and Conscious Choice, The West*

Moving around these four windows correlates well with the journey around the four directions of the Medicine Circle. The process of transformation moves clockwise around the cells just as the journey of healing and transformation moves sunwise around the Medicine Circle.

Cell I, *I Don't Know That I Don't Know*, represents the general state of unawareness most people find themselves in. It is standing at the East of the Circle, outside of it, unaware of its possibilities. It is the *La-La Land* of victimhood and denial. Those in this state are reacting to life. Their choices are driven by their circumstances. They see life as happening to them, by chance, and feel at the mercy of their circumstances. They are unaware that they interpret their experiences and make their choices through a filter of childhood paradigm. They actually believe that the Reality *they perceive* is real for everyone. Their relationships struggle over being Right about perceptions. The focus in this box is on the past: fear, guilt, shame, resentment, anger, blame, revenge, habit.

In Cell II, *I Know That I Don't Know*, we sense there is more to life. In its recognition, it represents active engagement at the East of the Circle. Illumination brings acknowledgment of opportunity. In its commitment to action, it moves toward the South of the Circle. We begin to see some patterns in our life experiences. Our attention is drawn to people who seem to have their lives together. We seek enlightenment and personal growth. We begin to take risks and engage with **Eagle** and **Porcupine**. We become aware that alternatives and options exist in experiencing life. We begin to pay attention to **Wolf** teaching us of causes and effects. Accepting our humanity begins to seem possible. It contains hope that perhaps I really am OK and that Empowerment is possible, even for me.

Cell III, *I Know That I Know*, is the most difficult one in terms of our experience of the journey. It is the West, where most people who quit the journey actually bail out. We have become aware of principles that work in life. We are consciously striving to apply them in our lives. It is hard work! We are acutely aware of our failings in that effort; habits of believing and choosing are not easy to change. And *we beat on ourselves.* "There I go again; I should know better!" In our conscious effort to live the principles, we have accepted total responsibility for our lives, swinging the pendulum from being victims of people and circumstances *to the other extreme* where we become victims of ourselves! We blame ourselves for everything that goes wrong in life. **Owl** seems to be our constant companion. We are faced with the constant struggle to confront and deal with our old belief system and our old habits of thinking and choosing. Every time those old beliefs assert themselves and we succumb, it seems to reinforce that maybe we were right after all! In Cell III we are making *conscious* choices to feel and do differently. It requires constant *and conscious* vigilance and energy. It is the West of the Circle where **Bear**, **Crow**, and **Owl** reign. In Cell III the medicine of **Eagle** (Spirit and Courage) and **Elk** (Stamina and Hanging-in-There) are most critical. It is the West of the Circle, the place where intense personal development work is actually done.

Cell IV, *I Don't Know That I Know*, is the stage of real Paradigm Shift. The principles have become *subconscious* and *habitual*. The way we look at ourselves and our world has really and truly changed, down inside. We really own it all, deep within, at a core place. We find ourselves making more resourceful choices and acting in new and more effective ways, *spontaneously.* After making some spontaneous choice, we *look back* on positive results with the recognition and realization that they actually flowed from a different paradigm. Our old way has truly shifted. Life has been transformed. There is much Satisfaction. We experience being Empowered. The spirits of **Moose** and **Buffalo** fill us with self-esteem and gratitude. We continually awaken to the realization *(in retrospect!)* that we are living in the North of the Circle. The focus in this cell is on the present where choice and learning reside. The Adult is now in charge of life.

Actually, the circle is a never ending journey. We embark on the journey and arrive in the North, in Cell IV, at some given stage of life, with respect to some specific issues of life. Invariably **Owl** will visit us again as life progresses, calling attention to some new stage or some new issue, and we see that the Medicine Circle Journey is really a spiral; so we return to the East and take on the next opportunity to learn and grow. The Empowered Life looks forward with excitement and anticipation to the upward journey around and around the Medicine Circle. The Empowered Life finds its joy and satisfaction in the journey, playing to win, seeking expansion and growth. Bring it on!

Where to from here?

When I first began writing this book back in 2003, I simply wanted to capture some things I had learned about life and get them into a form where they might be preserved for my posterity. In the years since that first edition, my own journey has continued. Nearly a decade of aging, of more grey hairs, and of experiencing life has passed since then. I have come to appreciate even more why those tribal people wanted their elders to teach their children. Learning in life never stops and the opportunities that life provides for that learning keep on coming.

I have had the opportunity to continue facilitating Ropes Courses and Firewalks. And I have had the opportunity to teach at a local community college, developmental math, arithmetic and algebra to college students who didn't learn it in elementary and secondary school. Both of these have added to what I continue to learn from the experiences of life. Education is never finished!

As I look toward the future, and consider the world my children and grandchildren will have to face and prepare for, I have recalled an idea I heard several years ago. The body of knowledge that humankind possesses, all the knowledge humanity has gained through experience with the world and study of it has grown, along with our technological development. This knowing represents human achievement and it grows along what has been called the Doubling Curve of Human Knowledge. That is, the sum of human knowledge doubles every so many years. The idea of a doubling rate of human knowledge is worth considering, for it is a real phenomenon and has serious implications for how you, and your children and posterity, will have to prepare for the future.

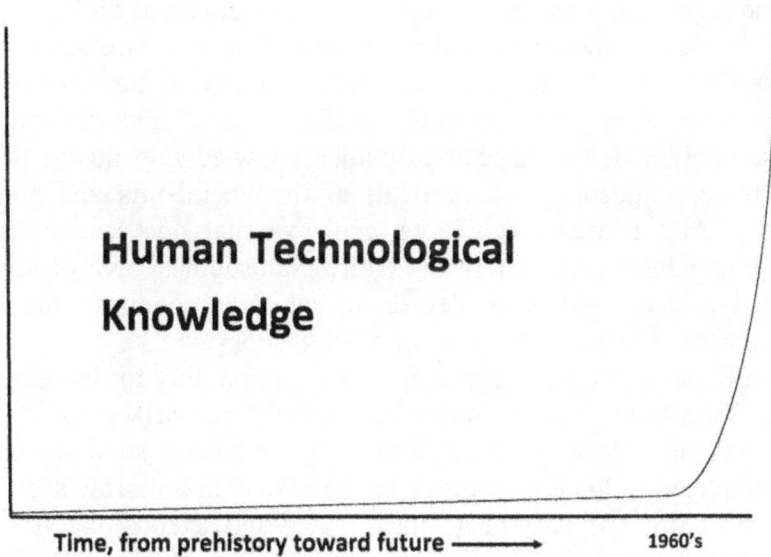

Human Technological Knowledge

Time, from prehistory toward future ———➤   1960's

Going back to prehistory, human technological knowledge had to comprehend fire and stone tools. Knowledge increased with the use of metals and writing. Simple mathematics, the wheel, astronomy, art— all represent increases in human knowledge. By some measures of this increase, it was fairly linear, increasing gradually for millennia, doubling in terms of millennia and centuries.

Then we came to the twentieth century and the Second World War. Jet engines, rocketry, computers. I was born into the planet during this amazing time. Knowledge increased at a more rapid rate through the Second World War and leading up to the 1960s when mankind achieved the ability to leave this earth and actually stand on another world. The 1960s changed the growth curve of human knowledge forever. Humanity passed through what mathematicians call an *inflection* in the growth curve of knowledge. Instead of rising fairly regularly, it began to zoom upward at an exponential rate!

Human knowledge is now increasing at an exponential rate, doubling every few years instead of every few centuries. And even that exponential doubling rate *is accelerating!* It is increasing so fast that what we know *becomes obsolete within one's career*. It is no longer possible to prepare for a career with stable knowledge and skills.

In the first millennium of the Common Era, what we sometimes call the Dark and Middle Ages, the degrees offered by the universities of the time were four: divinity, medicine, law, and philosophy. Philosophy included all aspects of human knowledge exclusive of the other three. Philosophy included all of the liberal arts and natural sciences. And it was possible to conceive that one person could achieve an education covering the entire philosophical area of human knowledge. The historical degree of Ph.D. recognized such an achievement of learning, the Doctor of Philosophy.

The Renaissance basically ended such a possibility for learning. In modern education, it is no longer possible for one person to hope to cover even all aspects of human knowledge in narrow subdivisions of it. I completed a Ph.D. in geology in the 1960s, in a narrow specialty within a narrow specialty of geology. Today, no scientist can hope to learn even the body of knowledge in tiny slices of specialty fields. Knowledge is increasing so fast that this year's newly discovered knowledge in some fields is obsolete by next year! Some kinds of new products are introduced faster than the old products' warranties expire!

The point here is: as you and your posterity contemplate the question, What Do I Want?, the answer, as far as preparing for the future is concerned, must take into account the exponential growth of knowledge and the fact that any current state of knowledge and skill will become obsolete well before a career is over, in some fields even before education in that field is finished!. The key to the future is not what you know or the skills you have, *but your ability to learn, your love of ongoing learning, and your ability to be flexible in dealing with a rapidly changing world.* This may be the most important mirror you can look into as we go forward into the twenty first century.

So how are you doing? How is your journey? What have you learned? About yourself? About your goals and aspirations? About your relationships? About yourself in relationship? About your emotional and spiritual health? Where to from here for you?

The Empowered Life is always asking questions. Questions that examine *what is* and direct one forward, toward *what can be*. If you haven't written down an inventory of what is in your life, it might be a good time to do it, before you put this book down. An honest, forthright, penetrating inventory of what you have in your life right now. Everything, the good, the bad, the ugly.

For this inventory, use the worksheets in the following section. Ask for feedback from *true friends* to get a broader picture of your present reality. You have in your life now exactly what you paid the price to have. Start a penetrating search for what you really want, more than anything, so much that you are willing to do Whatever-It-Takes to get it. Write it down. Tell your family and friends. In fact don't be reluctant to tell anyone who will listen what it is that you will pay any price to achieve in your life! They will know by the glint in your eye, the confident tone in your voice, and the spring in your step that you know who you are and accept full responsibility for everything, including accomplishing your dream. Then live with that glint, that voice, that step, and go forth to leave your mark on the world.

Empowerment is not an outcome or a destination. It is the fuel that powers the journey. Empowerment energizes the fuel tanks of your life when you get the principles and decide to live from them. And the world is thereafter blessed by your presence in it!

-Notes to Self-

Section Six—
My Personal Life
Inventory Worksheets

What I Have Now

What Do I Want?

What Price Am I Willing To Pay To Have It?

My Personal Life Inventory—

What I Have Now

Get Real! This is what you have been willing to pay the price to have! This is what you have bought with the efforts and choices of your life so far. Total self-honesty is the only path to true Empowerment. Check your self-honesty by asking for feedback on what you write here from your *true friends*.

Health

Relationships

      Spouse/Partner

      Children

      Parents

      Friends

      Siblings

      Extended family

      Professional

      Social

      Enemies

Education

Career

      Income

      Position

      Enjoyment

      Opportunities for growth and advancement

Possessions

      Home

      Transportation

      Furnishings

      Heritage

Spiritual Life

Plan for Future Security

      Investments

      Savings

      Insurance

      Will

Leisure and Recreation

      Hobbies

      Activities enjoyed and engaged in

      Shared

The things I don't like

The responsibilities I shirk

The debts I owe

The legal difficulties I have

Keep on going! It's your life. Get Real and get it all down! Keep this handy and add to it as you think of things from day to day.

What Do I Want?

What Price Am I Willing to Pay?

Take each category in the inventory above and Get Real about *what you really want* regarding that category. Be careful, because under each declaration, also put down the **price you are willing to pay** to have it in your life! And <u>by when</u> *you want to have it!* Remember, if you want something different than you have, you must be willing to pay a different price! Don't kid yourself! Serious and honest consideration of the price you will be paying will be a check on how much you really want it! Note especially the *if onlys* that show up in your thinking about each category. And remember, all the prices required will have to fit into a balanced life! Check with the significant people in your life to get *buy-in and support*. Remember, in Empowered and equal relationships, **they** are entitled to **your** buy-in and support, too! It is *Win/Win* or *No Deal*.

Health

Relationships

>   Spouse/Partner

>   Children

>   Parents

>   Friends

>   Siblings

>   Extended family

>   Professional

>   Social

>   Enemies

Education

Career

    Income

    Position

    Enjoyment

    Opportunities for growth and advancement

Possessions

    Home

    Transportation

    Furnishings

    Heritage

Spiritual Life

Plan for Future Security

    Investments

    Savings

    Insurance

    Will

Leisure and Recreation

    Hobbies

    Activities enjoyed and engaged in

    Shared

The things I don't like

The responsibilities I shirk

The debts I owe

The legal difficulties I have

Keep on going! It's your life. It's your dreams. Get Real and get it all down! Keep this handy and add as you think of things from day to day and as your life evolves into the future.

Using this inventory takes guts, because it is a perfect mirror. It will reveal to you the truth. You will have to face the reality of what you Really Want. For every "Whatever-It-Takes" price you tell yourself you are willing to pay, you must watch yourself closely as you consider the consequences of paying the price or are faced with the reality of actually paying the price. Listen closely to the little voices within, especially the ones that begin to rationalize. **You will hear them!** "I am willing to pay any price, *except. . . .if only. . . .unless. . . .*"

Every "except," "if only," "unless," reveals something that is <u>more important</u> to you than what you said you wanted. You see, the bottom line is simple. What you have right now is what you *have wanted!* What you have in your life right now is what you have been willing to pay the price to have. To have something different, you must be willing to pay a different price. You must establish different priorities. And the habits of price-paying around which you have invested in developing your life so far are the habits you will be breaking as you redirect your life to different results. A truly Empowered Life is never finished with the inventory. The inventory today is simply a *status report* in the ongoing process of personal growth and refinement, the upward journey that continues throughout life, the climbing spiral of the journey around the Medicine Wheel.

Sometimes the truth we have to face is tough truth. What I *kid myself into believing I want* is just not real for me. It is a self-deception, a pipe dream.

When I am faced with the price I will have to pay to have it, I may discover that I am not really willing to pay the price. It is not wrong to admit that. It is not a sign of weakness to redirect one's energy. Priorities are a personal choice. Getting real is not being wrong. It is coming out of deception!

One of the great rewards for a committed journey of life is the eventual discovery of who one really is and what one's gifts really are. With that discovery comes a welling-up of life energy to enable the gifts to truly be expressed and given to the world. In that realization comes a clearer vision of what one really wants, for it is consistent with who one really is. Then Whatever-It-Takes has clear and real meaning.

And now you get to live your dream. The price you are *Really* willing to pay will allow you to get very clear on what you really want. There is no right way or wrong way to live your life. There is only the way you choose to live it. And those choices will determine what kind of life's experiences and what kind of life's results you will have, for the rest of it!

In the journey of life, you either get Empowered or you die, whichever comes first.

God speed on your journey!

How to Contact Us

- For copies of this book and empowerment products
- For information about Empowerment Workshops and Support Groups
- For information about individual Empowerment Facilitation and Coaching
- For information about the Ropes Course or Firewalking

L. Cameron Mosher, Ph.D.

CAM MOSHER AND ASSOCIATES, INC.

P.O. Box 331, Sandy, Utah 84091-0331

801-243-7404 FAX 800-305-9908

www.IWalkedOnFire.com

cam@cammosher.com

www.ingramcontent.com/pod-product-compliance
Lightning Source LLC
Chambersburg PA
CBHW031834090426
42741CB00005B/241